French Colonists and Exiles
in the United States

French Colonists and Exiles in the United States

J. G. Rosengarten

Author of " The German Soldier in the Wars of the
United States," etc.

CLEARFIELD

Originally published
Philadelphia, 1907

Reprinted for
Clearfield Company, Inc. by
Genealogical Publishing Co., Inc.
Baltimore, Maryland
2002

International Standard Book Number: 0-8063-5144-6

Made in the United States of America

Contents

CHAPTER   PAGE

I. EARLY FRENCH SETTLEMENTS IN THE UNITED STATES 13

II. FRENCH COLONIES IN LOUISIANA 35

III. THE HUGUENOT SETTLERS 52

IV. FRENCH SOLDIERS IN THE UNITED STATES.. 64

V. EARLY FRENCH TRAVELLERS IN THE UNITED STATES 78

VI. FRENCH EXILES IN THE UNITED STATES.... 86

VII. FRENCH SETTLERS AND EXILES IN SOUTH CAROLINA 91

VIII. FRENCH SETTLEMENTS IN THE WEST AND IN CANADA 97

IX. BRILLAT SAVARIN IN THE UNITED STATES .. 103

X. FRENCH LAND COMPANIES IN THE UNITED STATES 106

XI. FRENCH PLAN OF EDUCATION IN THE UNITED STATES 121

XII. FRENCH COLONIES IN THE UNITED STATES: GALLIPOLIS, OHIO; ASYLUM, PENNA..... 125

XIII. FRENCH SETTLEMENT IN IOWA............ 151

XIV. BONAPARTIST EXILES 159

XV. ROYALIST EXILES 176

XVI. BALZAC'S STORY OF A FRENCH EXILE...... 183

XVII. FRENCH MEMBERS OF THE AMERICAN PHILOSOPHICAL SOCIETY..................... 186

APPENDIX A 211

APPENDIX B 220

INDEX 225

Introduction

THE French settlers in the United States have not received the attention due to them. Parkman and Bancroft and Roosevelt have dwelt upon the early history of the French in this country, and Fortier has given us an admirable work on the history of Louisiana. Many French authors and travellers have written about the United States, but little attention has been paid to the colonies settled with more or less success in the closing years of the Eighteenth and the beginning of the Nineteenth Centuries. Some accounts are found in local publications, those of state historical societies or in the pamphlets written by local authors, but these are not easily accessible. M. Anatole Le Braz, well known for his books on Brittany, suggested that a collected story be given of the efforts to establish French colonies in the United States. To do this I have made notes from the recognized historians, and from such

INTRODUCTION

local publications as could best serve to supply
information on the subject. There are some
references in the writings of travellers, and
especially of those of the numerous French
exiles who at the time of the French Revolution, and after the fall of Napoleon, visited
this country. These I have noted, too, as help-
ing to give an account of the French colonies
in the United States, as they saw them.

Philadelphia, as the political and social
capital, attracted these exiles, and many of
them made it their home. Some of them were
men of letters and of science, and were elected
members of the American Philosophical
Society, which thus had a close connection with
the most noted of the French settlers and colonists, while many distinguished French travellers were welcomed at its meetings, elected
members, and interested in its work. A brief
summary from its records will show how long
this connection lasted. Nearly all the early,
and many of the later French diplomatic representatives in this country were elected members, and the present distinguished French
Ambassador, M. Jusserand, well known by his

scholarly writings on English Literature
and its history, has received this acknowledgment, as well as due honors from many American universities.

The Huguenot settlers in the United States
have received exhaustive treatment in Baird's
History of the Huguenots, but even his industry did not follow them in all their settlements,
in Pennsylvania and elsewhere. Many later
French settlers have been absorbed into their
older neighbors; even names have been changed,
so as to make it difficult to recognize the original French patronymics. Of the comparatively recent French Socialist colonies in the
West little is known. It is hardly feasible to
say why the French colonies have never succeeded, while other settlers, Welsh, German,
Scotch, Irish, and in later times, Scandinavians,
Dutch and Italians, have persevered and become noteworthy factors in that great amal-
gam, the American people. Of the individual
French settlers many have achieved success,
and their names are known through the work
of their descendants, in art and science, in literature, in learned professions,—indeed, in

every walk of life our citizens of French birth and descent have proved a valuable addition. Of those less fortunate early French colonists, it is plain that their failure was largely due to American greed in land schemes.

Senator Lodge's *Century* (September, 1891) article on " The Distribution of Ability in the United States," reprinted in his " Historical and Political Essays " (Boston, 1892), gives a very high standard to the French, including the Huguenot Protestant French who came here during the Seventeenth and Eighteenth Centuries, either direct from France, or by way of England and Holland, and the French descendants of the original settlers in Louisiana, Missouri, and Illinois, of soldiers who came with Rochambeau, or refugees who fled here from France and from St. Domingo in 1792. He gives in his Division of Races, based on Appleton's Encyclopedia of American Biography, Huguenot 589, French 85, among statesmen, soldiers, clergy, lawyers, physicians, literary men, artists, scientists, educators, sailors, business men, philanthropists, pioneers and explorers, inventors, engineers, architects, musicians, actors. He says: "If we add the French and the French Huguenots together, we find that the people of French blood exceed absolutely, in the ability produced, all the other races represented in Appleton's Encyclopedia of American Biography, except the English and Scotch-Irish, and show a percentage in proportion to their total original immigration much higher than that of any other race." This is very high authority, and may well be accepted as a reason for a somewhat fuller recital of the contemporaneous history of the early, as well as of the later French colonies in the United States. Many names illustrious in French history will be found among those of the exiles who found refuge in the United States in the successive changes in France from the outbreak of the French Revolution, through the Napoleonic Period, the Bourbon restoration, the reign of Louis Philippe, the Second Republic, the Third Empire, and the Third Republic.

Pierre Leroy Beaulieu, in his exhaustive account of the United States in the Twentieth

Century (Paris, 1905), gives the number of French emigrants who came to the United States from 1821 to 1903, as 414,197. This number, though small as compared to the accessions of other nationalities, must be increased by the earlier settlements, those in Louisiana and up the valley of the Mississippi, and in Virginia and Pennsylvania; by those in Pennsylvania and Ohio after the French Revolution, and by the later refugees after the fall of Napoleon—a large number in all.

French Colonists and Exiles in the United States

I

EARLY FRENCH SETTLEMENTS IN THE UNITED STATES

THE oldest permanent European settlement in the valley of the Mississippi is the village of Kaskaskia; the seat of a Jesuit mission in 1684, it gradually became a central point of French civilization.[1] In Illinois La Salle opened the way, in 1681, and was followed by Tonti in 1700, with twenty Canadian settlers. In June, 1701, Cadillac was sent with one hundred French to settle Detroit, the oldest permanent settlement in Michigan. D'Iberville in 1698 opened direct intercourse between France and the Mississippi with two hundred settlers, and in 1699 his brother, Bienville, began the settle-

[1] Bancroft: Hist. U. S., vol. iii, p. 195.

ments near Mobile. Coxe, the proprietor of Carolana, on the Gulf of Mexico, obtained from King William permission to send six hundred French refugees and Vaudois to settle there. In 1698 Coxe sold 500,000 acres of his grant on the Gulf, to Sir William Waller, the Marquis de la Muce, and the Sieur de Sailly, on condition that at least two hundred Protestant colonists should be planted there within two years.

William III advanced £3,000 to defray the expenses of sending to Virginia at least five hundred French Protestants under the care of Coxe, and successive vessels brought them with their clergymen, to Manakintown, on the James, but the emigrants were soon in a deplorable state, and the enterprise was shortly abandoned. Coxe's son published in London, in 1722,[2] his Description of Carolana. Their title continued until 1769, when the family surrendered the charter of Carolana and received in exchange 100,000 acres of land in New York, and the township of Carolana and other patents were located in New York under

[2] Scull's Coxe: Pa. Mag. of History, vol. vii, p. 317.

this grant. Vincennes was settled at least as early as 1735, and thus began the commonwealth of Indiana.

In 1717, eight hundred emigrants for Louisiana began what was hoped to be a colony of at least six thousand whites, but in 1727 of Law's great colony only thirty needy Frenchmen were found, abandoned by their employer. In 1736 Alabama was opened to settlers at a heavy sacrifice of life.

It was on the banks of the Mississippi, in 1768, that uncontrolled impulses first unfurled the flag of a republic.[3] The treaty of Paris left two European powers sole sovereigns of the continent of North America. Spain, accepting Louisiana with some hesitation, lost France as the bulwark of her possessions, and assumed new expenses and new dangers, with only the negative advantage of keeping the territory from England. Its inhabitants were of French origin, and loved the land of their ancestry; by every law of nature and human freedom, they had the right to protest against the transfer of their allegiance. No sooner

---

[3] Bancroft: Hist. U. S., vol. vi, p. 217.

did they hear of the cession of their country to the Catholic king, than in the spirit of independence an assembly sprang into being, representing every parish in the colony, and they resolved unanimously to entreat the King of France to be touched with their affliction and their loyalty, and not to sever them from his dominions. At Paris their envoy, with Bienville, the time-honored founder of New Orleans, a venerable octogenarian, appealed in vain to Choiseul. In March, 1766, Ulloa landed in New Orleans. The French garrison of three hundred refused to enter the Spanish service; the people, to give up their nationality. This state of things lasted for two years, agitating the colony from one end to the other. It was proposed to make of New Orleans a republic, with a legislative body of forty men and a single executive. The people in the country parishes met together, crowded in a mass into the city, joined those of New Orleans, and formed a numerous assembly. They adopted an address, rehearsing their griefs, and in their Petition of Rights they claimed freedom of commerce with the ports of France and America; the inhabitants of Louisiana took up the idea of a republic, as the alternative to their renewed connection with France. Their hope was to be a colony of France or a free commonwealth. " A good example for the English colonies," wrote du Châtelet to Choiseul, " may they set about following it."

At this time Kaskaskia had six hundred whites, Cahokia, three hundred; Illinois about one thousand in all; Vincennes in Indiana about three hundred; Detroit about six hundred; New Orleans, eighteen hundred. The arrival of the Spanish squadron of twenty-four vessels with three thousand troops ended in the severe punishment of those who had led in the movement against Spain. The estates of twelve of the richest and most considerable men in the Province were confiscated, five were condemned to be hung, six to imprisonment.

Parkman in his great works, and since then countless writers, have described the great achievements of the early French explorers, La Salle, Champlain, Marquette, Joliet. La Salle's

Belle Rivière of 1670 was the Allegheny and Ohio, and Celeron de Bienville, sent by Galissoniere, commandant of forces in New France and Louisiana, in 1749, was the first European to sail on the waters of the Ohio.

La Salle in 1682 buried at the mouth of the Mississippi, a metal plate with the arms of France, as an emblem of sovereignty by right of discovery. In 1749 Celeron did the same thing at the confluence of the Ohio and Conowango, near what is now Warren, Pennsylvania, and near the mouths of French Creek in what is now Pennsylvania, and of Wheeling Creek and the Great Kanawha, in the West Virginia of to-day, and of the Muskingum and Great Miami Rivers in Ohio. The English in turn granted 500,000 acres on the Allegheny and Ohio Rivers to the Virginia Company in 1767.

It was in surveying this land that Washington first made his mark. The grave of Jumonville, killed in a skirmish by Washington's force, is still marked near Uniontown, Pennsylvania. That skirmish, between thirty-four men under Washington and thirty-one Frenchmen, was the opening of the Old French War, which finally cost France both Canada and the Ohio basin.

Roosevelt's "Winning of the West" tells the story of the men who finally settled that great region and made it part of the United States. As late as 1778 the French in Vincennes, learning that France was the ally of the United States in the war with Great Britain, helped George Rogers Clark in his gallant and successful invasion of the great West, which he helped to wrest from the mother country for the infant republic. But of the lesser French settlements and of the individual Frenchmen who came to this country, in some instances as travellers and visitors, often as exiles, there is little record.

The next colony located within the present State of Ohio was that of Gallipolis, settled directly from France.[4] This colony of about four hundred persons, had been made up in Paris, where the principal persons had pur-

---

[4] History of the Discovery and Settlement of the Valley of the Mississippi, by John W. Monette (New York, 1846, 2 vols.), vol. ii, p. 258, etc.

chased a large body of lands from Joel Barlow, agent of the Scioto Company. They had paid for their lands at the rate of a French crown per acre, while in France, to enable the Company to consummate their contract with the government. The agent of the Company had accompanied them to the Ohio River, and had selected for them a beautiful site on the west bank, two miles below the Great Kanawha River, and within the limits, as was subsequently ascertained, of the Ohio Company's purchase. The location having been selected, the immigrants remained upon the Ohio River, whither they had arrived from Philadelphia during the winter, ready to commence their new settlement.

Early in March, 1791, the colony was all action and enterprise, clearing land and erecting houses and inclosures for their future security from Indian hostility. Peace and joy seemed to smile upon them, and the arduous toil of the day was beguiled by mirth and festivity at night, cheered by the melody of the violin and the gay dance. But soon they found themselves deceived in a strange land, beset by savage foes, and in fact without a home and without money. The Scioto Company could not give titles to the land and was not responsible for the one hundred thousand francs they had received from the credulous Frenchmen. These were without a remedy. Many of them left the country; others received from Congress a grant of 24,000 acres near the Scioto, known as the French Grant; others migrated to the Wabash, to join their countrymen at Vincennes; some returned to Philadelphia and then to France.[5]

" Historic Illinois: The Romance of the Earlier Days," by Randall Parrish, Chicago, 1905, is a compilation of information on the early settlements in Illinois. By 1712 the French population had increased to considerable proportions, most largely concentrated at Kaskaskia. By 1763 the Jesuits there had a church, a chapel, a house, all built of stone, a plantation of two hundred and forty arpents of land, well stocked with cattle, and a brewery. All was seized under the edict of their expulsion

---

[5] American Pioneer, vol. i, pp. 94, etc.; vol. ii, pp. 182, etc.; Atwater's Ohio, p. 159.

from France, and but little left of the results of their hundred years of devotion to the task undertaken by them.

The old trails led from Kaskaskia to the Peorias, at the mouth of the Des Moines River, and to Detroit, part of the latter still a legal highway in continual use. Later Clark laid out one to Fort Massac on the Ohio River, thus avoiding the old French trail.

The establishment, in 1682, by La Salle, of Fort St. Louis attracted adventurous Frenchmen, coureurs de bois, voyageurs, soldiers, fur traders, and priests, but with the abandonment of the post in 1702 they soon scattered. The oldest permanent settlement, not only in Illinois, but in the entire Mississippi valley, was that of Kaskaskia, "Notre Dame de Cascasquias,"—first an Indian village, then a missionary station, then slowly gathered a vagrant white population. By 1766 there were about one hundred families, French and English, many of the original French inhabitants having gone to St. Louis. Most of the settlers of Kaskaskia came from New Orleans, those of Cahokia from Canada; Prairie du Rocher, fourteen miles from Kaskaskia, grew up about Fort Chartres. The names of some of the earliest colonists of Illinois are preserved in the records at Quebec.

The early histories of Illinois describe their homes,—they were largely descendants from emigrants from Picardy and Normandy. In 1720 Major Pierre Dugue Boisbriant, some of whose descendants yet reside at Prairie du Rocher, accompanied by one hundred men, came up from New Orleans, and sixteen miles from Kaskaskia built Fort Chartres. In 1721 Renault brought two hundred miners and five hundred slaves to work the mines he expected to discover. In 1745 the Illinois country sent 400,000 pounds of grain to New Orleans, the surplus product of a population of about nine hundred all told.

At Kaskaskia, Cahokia, Prairie du Rocher, Prairie du Pont, and St. Philippe, the peasantry in their picturesque costumes, conspicuous with coloring, mingled with gentlemen who, even in that wilderness, clung to the Parisian garb, with the French soldiers in their blue uniforms and white facings, the black-robed Jesuits, and the stolid Indian warriors. After 1721 black slaves were numerous throughout the settlements. These were originally St. Domingo negroes brought by Renault to labor in his mines, but twenty years later sold to the colonists. In 1750 there were five French villages with eleven hundred whites, three hundred blacks, and sixty savages. At Le Pé, now Peoria; at Chicago, possibly at Rock Island and Quincy, there were small stockaded forts with a few French settlers. A trading-post was established on the Missouri side of the river at New Madrid as early as 1740. The region was notable for bears, and the principal trade was the sale of bear's grease, hence the name, L'Anse de la Graisse. The fortified trading-post of Vincennes was established in 1722, but did not become a French settlement until twelve years later. These isolated communities furnished many French volunteer soldiers.

Thus flourished for nearly a hundred years these communities of French pioneers. They accomplished little of permanent value. Their forts have crumbled into dust; their towns have disappeared beneath the encroaching waters

or have decayed and passed away; only a few
remnants have escaped the inflowing tide of
American population, and they also are fast
losing the peculiarities of their fathers. In
1791 by special act of Congress four hundred
acres of land were granted to each head of a
family who had made improvements in Illinois
prior to 1788. A list of names of those entitled shows two hundred and forty-four, of
whom eighty were Americans, the others
French. Allowing five to a family, this would
make eight hundred and twenty. In 1791
under the militia law there were two hundred
and twenty-five Frenchmen capable of bearing
arms.

Renault, St. Philippe, Prairie du Rocher,
Fort Chartres, Massac, Kaskaskia, Cahokia,
Fort St. Louis, Fort Crèvecœur, are names that
still reveal the sites of early French settlements
in Illinois, while Father Allouez, Aubry, Bar-
beau, Barbier, Baugy, Beausoleil, Bellefon-
taine, Bienville, Noel Blanc, Boilvin, Boisron-
det, Bossu, Bourdon, Bouthillier, Brossard,
Chevet, De Montbrun, Du Page, Galland, Ger-
main, Guyon, La Forest, La Grange, Le

Comte, Meillet, Membré, Menard, Moreau, Pachot, Saussier, are a few of the French names of individuals who reveal the French element in Illinois.

Roosevelt's " Winning of the West " [New York, 1894] has many suggestive references to early and later French settlements.[6]

Mobile in 1781 was described by an early French traveller (Le Gal, Paris, 1802) as a little terrestrial paradise, with about forty proprietary families.

In 1784 there were four hundred French families in the Illinois country, a like number at Vincennes, and four hundred and forty at Kaskaskia and Cahokia. In 1778 the British Governor, Hamilton, reported the number of settlers at Vincennes as six hundred and twenty-one.

Roosevelt describes the life of the French Creoles, and quotes Collot's account of them and of the great fur trade built up by one of them, Gratiot. The French settlers of the Illinois and Wabash country quarrelled with

---

[6] Roosevelt: " Winning of the West," vol. i, pp. 31, 35; vol. ii, pp. 39, 78.

the new American comers, whose energy disturbed their easy-going life. In 1786 Vincennes had upwards of three hundred houses, and sixty American families took refuge there from the hostile Indians. The old French families complained of the abuses inflicted on them in poor return for the hospitality extended to the refugees, and General Clark established a garrison of one hundred and fifty men of his command to keep order. To punish marauding Indians an attack was made on a settlement of French Indian traders in Cumberland County, Kentucky, in which the latter suffered for the help they had given the Indians. French and Americans alike suffered at the hands of the Spanish in their efforts to stop trade with New Orleans; some of the French moved to the west (Spanish) side of the Mississippi, to enjoy the benefit of their protection.

In 1787 there were five hundred and twenty French at Vincennes, one hundred and ninety-one at Kaskaskia, two hundred and thirty-nine at Cahokia, eleven at St. Philippe, seventy-eight at Prairie du Rocher, ten hundred and thirty-nine in all, or as another account put it, one thousand and forty French at the six villages on the Wabash and the Illinois, as against two hundred and forty Americans, of which one hundred and three were at Vincennes and one hundred and thirty-seven in the Illinois country.[7] Roosevelt quotes from a memorial of the French settlers to Congress for a confirmation of the titles to their lands; their agent Tardiveau, a French mercantile adventurer, had relations with the Spanish agents and the Kentucky separatists. General Harmar, in taking possession of Vincennes and the French towns, spoke well of the " Creoles," but said they could best be governed in the manner to which they were accustomed, by a commandant with a few troops. Sprung as they were from French soldiers, naturally they preferred a strong military rule. The American settlers were almost all soldiers of the Revolutionary armies,—hard-working, orderly men of trained courage and keen intellect, courteous, industrious and law-abiding. A fortnight after the

---

[7] Roosevelt: " Winning of the West," vol. iii, pp. 235, 237, 239, 263, 266, 272.

passage of the ordinance of 1787 for the government of the Northwest Territory, the Ohio Company bought a million and a half acres north of the Ohio, and three and a half millions more were authorized to be sold to the Scioto Company, nominally at seventy cents an acre, but as payment was made in depreciated public securities, the real price was only eight or nine cents an acre. Manasseh Cutler was the leader in these ventures, and on his first trip up the Ohio was cared for by a well-to-do Creole trader from the Illinois, Francis Vigo, who had welcomed Clark when he took Kaskaskia.

At a dinner given to the officers of Fort Harmar on July 4, 1787, one of the toasts was to the King of France. Even in the Indian wars, the Creoles suffered little at the hands of the savages. Clark had given the name of Louisville in honor of that king of France whose alliance, he hoped, would render easier the task of winning over the inhabitants of the Illinois, just as later on Marietta was so called in honor of Marie Antoinette and to allure the royalist exiles to Ohio. Earlier already Patrick Henry, Governor of Virginia, had advised Clark to secure the friendship of the French, and they stood him in good stead in rescuing the West from the British. This, too, made the French towns outposts for the protection of the settlers. Between the increasing flow from the old States and the attacks of the British with their French-Canadian and Indian allies, the old French settlements were in hard plight. Frenchmen were appointed to most of the civilian offices, while the military posts were under Americans. While Frenchmen, layman and priest, helped the Americans with money and goods, the French resorted to punishment of their negroes of such severity as to shock even the frontiersmen.

Genet's plans to organize an armed expedition on the Ohio River in 1793-4 to conquer Louisiana, as Spain was then an ally of England and at war with France, found support in the discontented adventurers of the West, led by General Clark.[8] Genet commissioned him as a major-general in the service of the French Republic, and sent out various Frenchmen,—

---

[8] Roosevelt: "Winning of the West," vol. iv, pp. 176, 182, 243, 268.

Michaux (nominally on a scientific tour of exploration), La Chaise, Collot, and others, with civil and military titles,—to coöperate with Clark, but the movement collapsed with Genet's recall. Clark tried to get reimbursement from the French government for the "expenses of expedition ordered by Citizen Genet," but of course without result.

In 1791 the most pitiable group of emigrants that reached the West at this time was formed by the French who came to the town of Gallipolis, on the Ohio. They were mostly refugees from the Revolution, who had been taken in by a swindling land company. They were utterly unsuited to life in the wilderness, being gentlemen, small tradesmen, lawyers, and the like. Unable to grapple with the wild life into which they found themselves plunged, they sank into shiftless poverty, not one in fifty showing industry and capacity to succeed. Congress took pity on them and granted them 24,000 acres in Scioto County, the tract being known as the French Grant; but no gift of wild land was able to insure their prosperity. By degrees they were absorbed into the neighboring communities, a few succeeding, most ending their lives in abject failure.

In 1800 Napoleon was planning for France the reëstablishment in America of that colonial empire which a generation before had been wrested from her by England. His great ambition halted at the tremendous sacrifice of French troops in the failure of the West-Indian military expedition, and the great demands of Bernadotte and Victor as the conditions on which they would undertake to establish a French imperial colony in Louisiana, Texas, and Mexico.

In " Mount Desert, a History," by Geo. E. Street, Boston, 1905, there is a brief sketch of the efforts towards French colonization by Roberval and La Roche, with reference to Winsor's " Cartier to Frontenac," and an account of the organized French colony on the St. Croix. The French plans of colonization were made under Henry IV, who in 1599 commissioned Pierre Chauvin to colonize America, and later gave a like commission to Du Guast, Sieur de Monts, set forth in Baird's " Huguenot Emigration to America," vol. i, pp. 341–7, and in Fiske's " New France and New England." The colony on Mount Desert was brought there in 1613, but it was of short duration. The only trace of it is in the names given by the French. In 1688 Mount Desert was granted to Cadillac by Louis XIV; he made a short stay there, going later to Mackinac and then to Detroit and finally to Louisiana as Governor, 1712-17, and leaving his name connected with points in eight of the present States of the Union. Parkman's " Frontenac " and Margry's " Relations et Mémoirs Inédits " give particulars of his active career. The Baron de St. Castine settled on the site of the present town of Castine, Maine, and left a family of half-breed children, who were driven off by the English, and all trace of them is lost after their return to France. In 1786 the Gregoires as descendants, on the wife's side, of Cadillac, obtained from Massachusetts a grant of land on the west side of Mt. Desert Island, settled at what is now called Hull's Cove, built a house and mill and began to farm. The husband died in 1810, the wife in 1811, and the children returned to France and were lost sight of. The

FRENCH COLONISTS AND EXILES

French colonies on Mt. Desert were short lived but are recalled there by the recently erected cross as a memorial of their landing at St. Sauveur. Their early explorations of the coast of New England have of late years been republished and their maps have an historical interest and are remarkably accurate.

II

French Colonies in Louisiana

Fortier's History of Louisiana is written by one whose family settled in New Orleans shortly after its foundation in 1718. He naturally takes pride in relating the history of the events on the soil of Louisiana for the last two hundred years, for in nearly all of them men of his name or blood took part. La Salle gave the name of Louisiana in 1679, in honor of Louis XIV, and in 1682 took formal possession in the king's name, planting a cross and burying a leaden plate with a record of the fact. He established Fort St. Louis among the Illinois, and after an interview with the King, brought out, in 1684, soldiers, mechanics, laborers, volunteers, several families, and a number of girls, his brother who was a Sulpician priest, with others of that order, and three Recollet friars. On his way from what is now Texas, where he landed by mistake

35

at Matagorda Bay, which he took for one of
the mouths of the Mississippi, to Canada, to
get help for his colony, he was killed by his
companions in 1687, thus wrecking his plans,
and leaving it for Iberville and Bienville to
found Louisiana. They landed in 1699, built
a fort, manned it, and named the two lakes
Maurepas and Pontchartrain, in honor of the
Ministers under whose auspices he had made
his expedition. A geologist, Lesueur, went
out in search of minerals. Iberville, on his
third and last voyage, found only one hundred
and fifty persons in the colony. More than
sixty had died. He sent his brother Bienville
to found another colony on Mobile River. In
1704 he reported one hundred and eighty men
bearing arms, twenty-seven French families,
some slaves, four ecclesiastics, eighty wooden
houses, nine oxen, fourteen cows, four bulls,
five calves, one hundred hogs, three goats, four
hundred chickens. A census of 1706 gives the
names of the settlers with the number of their
families, making eighty-two in all, and a list of
the cattle, forty-six head in all. In 1708 a
report gave the population as composed of a

garrison of one hundred and twenty-two persons, including priests, workmen and boys, one hundred and fifty-seven inhabitants, men, women, and children, besides sixty wandering Canadians and eighty Indian slaves, and fourteen hundred hogs, two thousand chickens, and about one hundred head of cattle.

In 1712 Louisiana was granted to Crozat for fifteen years, and Cadillac, the founder of Detroit, was made governor, but was soon removed. In 1717 the colony contained seven hundred, of all ages, sexes, and colors. In 1710 Mobile was founded, and in 1717 three companies of infantry and fifty settlers came. In that year Crozat surrendered his charter and the colony was given to John Law, who made it part of his Company of the Indies. In 1718 Bienville as governor, founded New Orleans. In 1721 the colony numbered about six thousand, including six hundred negroes. In 1722 New Orleans was made the capital, and Charlevoix said it had about one hundred huts, a large store, and a few other buildings, yet he predicted a brilliant future. Le Page du Pratz in his History of Louisiana (Paris,

1758), gives his own personal experience during his stay in the colony from 1718 to 1734. Dumont, who was twenty-two years in Louisiana, gave an account of the colony in his book, and the archives of the Colonial Office in Paris contain frequent census returns, showing the condition of the colony in 1721, 1723, 1726, 1727, and its increase in numbers and prosperity, in spite of Indian wars, mismanagement by the home government, and troubles of the local authorities. Then came the cession to Spain, in 1764, and in 1765 the French left Fort Chartres, in the territory ceded to Great Britain, crossed the Mississippi, and founded St. Louis, the first settlement of what is now Missouri. Then came the Acadians, refugees from British oppression, who in time became a source of wealth to Louisiana by their industry. L'Abbé Casgrain estimates their descendants as numbering one hundred thousand. With the cession to Spain, the colony lost its prosperity, and after fruitless appeals to France there was a short-lived revolution, for the population of less than twelve thousand, of whom half were slaves, could not resist the power of Spain. It gave Louisiana the glory of having thought of establishing a republican form of government in America in 1768, eight years before the Declaration of Independence. It ended in punishment of the leaders by death, imprisonment, exile, and confiscation, that left Spain unpopular.

Although under Spanish rule, Louisiana, through the successful campaign of Galvez against the English and his capture of Pensacola with the surrender of English and Waldeck troops, can proudly boast of having aided the Americans in the war for Independence of the United States. In 1785 a number of Acadians came to Louisiana at the expense of the King of France and were settled through the country. It was Boré, born at Kaskaskia, in the Illinois district, in 1741, of an old Norman family, educated in France at a military school, and settling in Louisiana in 1768, who successfully introduced the sugar industry there.

In 1798 Louis Philippe and his brothers visited New Orleans and were received with great cordiality, one of the richest men of the colony, Poydras, loaning them money. In

1800 Berthier, who had served under Rochambeau, made on behalf of Napoleon the treaty of St. Ildefonso, confirmed by a later treaty at Madrid signed by Lucien Bonaparte, by which Louisiana became again a French colony. Later, in 1803, Rochambeau (the son) surrendered St. Domingo to the blacks, and many exiles went to Louisiana, to join their friends who had already taken refuge there. Bernadotte was appointed captain-general of Louisiana, but as he demanded three thousand soldiers and as many agriculturists, Bonaparte declared he would not do as much for one of his brothers, appointed Bernadotte Minister to the United States, an office he declined, and General Victor was made captain-general and Laussat colonial prefect,—the former with a salary of 70,000 francs, the latter 50,000,—but the expedition to Louisiana was abandoned, Victor never sailed, and all he did was to draw his salary and issue a bombastic proclamation.

Pontalba, who left a memoir on Louisiana, was born in New Orleans in 1754, educated in France, served under Noailles and D'Estaing at the siege of Savannah in 1779, resigned and returned to New Orleans in 1784. Pontalba submitted to Napoleon a memoir on Louisiana, in which he said: " In the hands of France, the colony must be called to the most brilliant destiny, and be a source of riches for the metropolis. Almost all the Louisianians are born French or are of French origin. They would again become French with enthusiasm. The deficit of $337,000 will be covered in a few years merely by the progress of the sugar plantations. People it, it will become an inexhaustible source of wealth for France." This memoir, dated Paris, 29 Fructidor, year IX (September 15, 1801), was presented to General Bonaparte by Decrès, after the treaty of 1800 conveyed Louisiana back to France.

Laussat reached New Orleans in March, 1803, and issued a proclamation that said: " Your separation from France marks one of the most shameful epochs of her annals, under a government already weak and corrupt, after an ignominious war, and as the result of a shameful peace," and received a simple and dignified address in reply, signed by the principal inhabitants, followed by one from the planters, full of gratitude for the return to France. Yet on April 30, 1803, the treaty ceding Louisiana to the United States was signed in Paris. Laussat had denounced the report as an impudent and incredible falsehood to assist the partisans of Jefferson!

The transfer was made on November 30, 1803, with solemn ceremonies,—Laussat and the Spanish general exchanged civilities, and the former finally handed Louisiana over to the United States Commissioners on December 20, 1803. Napoleon was largely guided by Decrès, who had served in the French army in the American War of Independence, and Barbé Marbois, who had been the French diplomatic representative in this country, and had an American wife (Miss Moore of Chester County, Pennsylvania). He wrote a History of Louisiana and tells the story of Napoleon's decision, to enable him to wage war in Europe against England with American money.

Laussat left " Memoirs," printed at Paris in 1831, from which Professor Fortier has drawn much interesting material. The French flag was escorted by a company of fifty French citizens, who had served in the French army, from the beginning of the Revolution, and tears were shed when the French flag disappeared from the shores of Louisiana. There were some signs of hostility between French and Americans, but these soon ceased. Robin, who was also present, wrote a book in which he makes a record of his own observations of the cession, and his voyage to Louisiana is of interest and value from the period of his visit.

Professor Fortier gives the dates of the French settlements in the Illinois country and upper Louisiana: old Kaskaskia in the " terrestrial paradise " at the end of the Seventeenth Century; Fort Chartres in 1720, nearby Cahokia, Prairie du Rocher, etc., Kaskaskia with a college and monastery of the Jesuits in 1721, chartered in 1725; Vincennes in 1735; St. Louis in 1764, by Chouteau, with thirty men, increased in 1765 by families leaving the country ceded to the British. It remained practically French even after the cession to Spain.

Among the noteworthy Frenchmen who took

part in the battle of New Orleans was General Humbert, who was a brigadier in the French army, served in Vendée, was in 1798 commander-in-chief of the French expedition to Ireland, later took part in the unfortunate expedition to St. Domingo, lost the favor of Napoleon, came to New Orleans, where he taught school; in 1816 went to Mexico to fight for its independence, but was unsuccessful, and returned to New Orleans, where he died in 1823. Latour, of the French Polytechnic School, was one of the principal engineers of Jackson's army. Lefebvre, a soldier of the Republic under Bonaparte, served the mortars. General Moreau had suggested the points of defence. Lakanal, the conventionnel, was principal of the College of Orleans; he came to the city of New Orleans after the restoration of the Bourbons, proscribed as a regicide. Congress made him a grant of land, and he lived on a farm on Mobile Bay, until he returned to France, in 1837, where he died in 1845, honored for his work in science.

The Hunter Dunbar expedition up the Washita in 1804 found two large land grants located on the Washita, that of the Marquis de Maison Rouge and twelve leagues square above it, that of the Baron de Bastrop.

In 1804 Robin, a French traveller (he published his account in Paris in 1807), said the American government was doing nothing to advance American settlement. The forest Americans (backwoodsmen) were not comparable to the robust French as emigrants.[1] All the early American expeditions were materially helped by French settlers, trappers, etc. In 1805 two Frenchmen from Illinois, Lalande and Durocher, and later, in 1806, three more joined Pike's expedition and gave him much useful information.[2]

The Chouteau family enjoyed for twenty years the exclusive privilege (from the Spanish and French governments) of trading up the Osage River, before Pike came to the Osage country in 1806. It was through French traders that he learned of the safe return of Lewis and Clark to St. Louis from their epoch-

---

[1] Robin's Travels, vol. iii, p. 141.
[2] Cox: The Early Exploration of Louisiana, pp. 12, etc. University of Cincinnati Press, 1906.

making expedition. Perrin du Lac in his Travels says: In 1801 he found in Elizabeth-town, New Jersey, a number of French refugees from St. Domingo and Guadeloupe. Near Harrisburg he met a Frenchman who had been by turn, soldier, merchant, government employee, musician, and was earning his living as a dancing master.

At Gallipolis he found a hundred and sixty people, all that were left of six hundred families emigrated from France in 1790-91, only to find that the Scioto Company had sold them land to which it had no title. After four years of misery Congress gave them land sixty miles from Gallipolis, but most of the owners sold it for nominal prices, while a few remained in poverty at Gallipolis.

Perin says that it is due to the Baron de Carondelet, the Spanish governor of Louisiana, that acknowledgment be made him for his successful opposition to the establishment of the Inquisition, urgently solicited by the Bishop.

In "Louisiana: A Record of Expansion," by Albert Phelps (American Commonwealths, New York, 1905), there are references to the

" First French Settlements in Louisiana," and the foundation of Mobile in 1701 by Bienville under Iberville's orders, from Hamilton's " Colonial Mobile," and Margry's collections. It was under Law's vast grant and powers that the full tide began to reach Louisiana. The emigrants, hurried out to fill seignorial grants, began to arrive in swarms. The first three shiploads arrived in 1718. The colony responded to the European enthusiasm. In June three hundred colonists for the Mississippi arrived; one hundred and fifty-one of these were sent to the Natchez; eighty-two to the Yazoos, and sixty-eight to New Orleans. Ship after ship came in loaded with settlers; in August, 1718, there had arrived eight hundred in three ships, and among them Le Page du Pratz, the first historian of Louisiana. One hundred were sent to the Illinois, others to the Mississippi, to Bay St. Louis, Biloxi, and Mobile.

Later on, under Spanish rule, the governor, Carondelet, encouraged the immigration of French royalists fleeing from the horrors of the Revolution, welcoming them as an offset to the

Republicans, who, encouraged by " Citizen " Genet and his emissaries, from Philadelphia, had set on foot plans for the recapture of Louisiana for France. On the Washita (Ouachita) River he granted twelve square leagues to the Baron de Bastrop; thirty thousand acres to the Marquis de Maison Rouge, and ten thousand square arpents to De Lassus and St. Vrain. These concessions were not settled by the proprietors, but they were destined to play a part in the famous scheme of Aaron Burr some years later. In 1797 Carondelet was made uneasy by the presence of the French General Collot, who had been making maps and plans and inspecting the miniature forts near New Orleans. He arrested Collot and sent him to Philadelphia on the rumor that France was eager to regain Louisiana and that Collot had been sent to reconnoitre the ground.

Gayarré in " A Louisiana Sugar Plantation of the Old Régime " (*Harper's Magazine*, March, 1887), gives a complete picture of a typical Louisiana plantation in the old days before American control. It was the plantation of Etienne de Boré, the patron saint of Louisiana sugar planters. The table was free to every white traveller, even the humblest wayfarer. The Boré plantation was typical of all the large plantations of sugar, cotton, indigo, and tobacco.

The incident of the single attempt to establish the Holy Inquisition in Louisiana is typical of the kindly tolerance of the French Creoles. In 1789 the Spanish Capuchin Antonio de Sedella, under the new policy of the bigoted Carlos IV, was appointed emissary of the Inquisition to Louisiana. His portrait is in the Cathedral—a tall, gaunt figure. He had his agents and his implements of torture, and made his investigations with secrecy and caution. Apparently when his first victims had been chosen, he applied to Governor Miró for a file of soldiers that he might need. Miró sent the soldiers, not, however, to assist the Holy Office, but to arrest the representative of the Inquisition and pack him off to Spain, with a bold justification of his act, " lest the mere name of the Inquisition uttered in New Orleans would check immigration, which is successfully progressing, and would drive away those who have recently come." Father Sedella returned to Louisiana, and remained for many years the most beloved of priests; when he died, in 1829, the whole city mourned for him— hermit, saint, friend of the people.

In the War of 1812 Great Britain counted on the help of the great number of refugees from Jamaica, St. Domingo, Guadeloupe, and other West Indian islands. It was hoped they might be induced to assist the British invasion, and that the contraband traders and smugglers might be employed as effective auxiliaries. The latter, known by the general name of Baratarians, were daring men, refugees from the French West Indies, who under letters of marque from France and from the young republic of Carthagena, preyed upon British commerce as privateers. Some time about the year 1809 there had come to New Orleans from Bayonne or Bordeaux the brothers Pierre and Jean Lafitte. They were soon known as the chief agents of the Baratarian smugglers. Jean Lafitte acquired such an ascendency over them that his orders received instant obedience, while he maintained his place among the quiet citizens of New Orleans. Gayarré's Historical Sketch of Pierre and Jean Lafitte gives an exhaustive account of their strange career. Latour in his Historical Memoir confirms their services to General Jackson in his defence of New Orleans. He found the Baratarians men after his own heart, accepted Jean Lafitte's offer of trained gunners, and promised to obtain pardon for them from the President. They manned the forts, and the two chief batteries were given to Dominique Yon and Beluche, with their fellow pirates and some veteran gunners of the French army. General Humbert was one of Jackson's active aids. The victory of the 8th of January was thus largely due to Frenchmen and to the French Creoles, descendants of the early settlers, who thus attested their fidelity to the government of the United States.

III

THE HUGUENOT SETTLERS

BAIRD tells the sad story of the early attempt to settle a French colony in Florida, in the Seventeenth Century. Ribaut was chosen by Coligny to lead the first expedition. He landed near Beaufort, South Carolina; returning to France and entering the Huguenot ranks, he led, at the suggestion of Coligny, the third expedition, which ended in his murder by the Spaniards. Laudonniere led the second expedition, but was superseded by Ribaut.

Baird gives in great detail the names of the Huguenot refugees who sought and found shelter in the American colonies, from Maine to South Carolina. Many of the descendants are still found in the United States, often with names changed, yet easily recognizable. Among them were clergymen, men of education and attainments, some who had held important positions in France; others were mariners, merchants and tradesmen, and artisans, and their new home profited by their virtues.

Francis Marion, the brave soldier in the American War of Independence, was the worthy descendant of a Huguenot exile. Paul Revere is another Huguenot name famous in American heroic history. Faneuil Hall in Boston perpetuates another. Of others, the history of America has examples in famous soldiers and great sailors, in statesmen, in bishops and noted clergymen,—indeed, in every walk of life the descendants of Huguenots exiled to America have strengthened the historic ties between France and the United States.

The Le Contes have rendered notable services to natural science in successive generations. Rhode Island welcomed some of the Huguenot exiles, and Penn invited others to his province. All of the American colonies were anxious to secure the Huguenots as settlers, and they came both as individuals and in quite large bodies. In New Rochelle they secured a tract of land and built a church and endowed it with a glebe, and to this day the French language is used in the Huguenot Church in Charleston, South Carolina, in pious reverence.

Many hundreds, aided by generous grants from the crown, came to Virginia and suffered no little hardship from the unscrupulous landowners and speculators. Those who came to New England fared better, and more than returned by their prosperity the help extended to them. They were successful merchants and sturdy fighters and patriotic citizens, and names such as Bowdoin, Faneuil, and Revere, are typical of the addition to New England of the French Huguenots as an element of good in its growth and development.

A monument erected in 1884 perpetuates the memory of the Huguenot settlers in Oxford, then a frontier town in Massachusetts, and the story of their hardships is preserved in many records. It was not until 1721 that the settlement was finally broken up and its tract of twenty-five hundred acres sold. Of the settlers the Sigourneys, the Bowdoins, the Dupuys and others joined the families living elsewhere, and Hartford and New York and Newport and

New Rochelle welcomed this addition to their number.

The early settlers in East Greenwich, Rhode Island, in a locality still known as Frenchtown, were soon scattered by quarrels of the claimants for the land and by unfair treatment. Baird prints a " Mapp of the [lands of the] French Refugee Gentlemen who are all turned out by the Road Islanders," reproduced from the original prepared by Ayrault in a petition for redress, still in the British State Paper Office. Ayrault's name is perpetuated in a street in Newport, where his son removed. Others joined their fellow Huguenots in more flourishing colonies, but Providence and Bristol and Newport still bear in pious memory the good done by those who remained in Rhode Island. The story of the Huguenots in America, as told by Baird and in many local and family histories, is a very interesting and important chapter in the varied history of the French settlers in the United States. It shows how valuable an element was thus infused into the varied streams that have gathered together in the people of the great republic.

FRENCH COLONISTS AND EXILES

A French Protestant church was established in New York in the Seventeenth Century. French Huguenot refugees took up a tract of six thousand acres near that city, at New Rochelle, a name suggesting their old home in France. One hundred acres were set apart for the endowment of a church, and of the ninety members many of the names are still familiar in New York, while these again are often perpetuated in the streets of the city. In 1724 a quarrel in the Huguenot Church in New York became matter of record in its Documentary History, nearly a hundred men and women members of the congregation signing for one side, with only eight on the other, but these including the pasteur, l'Ansien [*sic*], and six of the consistory. In 1761–62 the members of the French Church at New Rochelle are on record as petitioners to Governor Colden, reciting that in 1681 their land was granted to them.[1]

---

[1] Registers of the Births, Marriages and Deaths of the French Church in New York from 1688 to 1804.— Collections of the Huguenot Society of New York, vol. i. New York, 1886.

The first French service was held in New
York in 1628. In 1623 thirty families of
Walloon or French came to the Delaware, to
Connecticut, and up the Hudson. Additions
came in 1625 and 1626, and between 1628 and
1638, and between 1648 and 1658. Many of
the descendants became leading citizens and
some of them important men in the history of
the United States.

Stapleton's " Memorials of the Huguenots
in America, with special reference to their
Emigration to Pennsylvania," Carlisle, Pennsylvania, 1901, is supplementary to Baird's
" Huguenot Emigration to America," and
mentions the contributions to a knowledge of
their settlements in Pennsylvania, Virginia,
New England, and South Carolina. In Charleston, South Carolina, their memory is kept alive
by the French service in the Huguenot Church.
In New York and in New England the names
of the Huguenot settlers are still familiar in
Bowdoin, Revere, and many others well known.
In Pennsylvania there were many settlers of
French Huguenot faith. The first distinct
settlement was that led by Mme. Ferree

to a large tract of land bought by her in Lancaster County in 1709. Her son and her son-in-law, Isaac Lefever, settled in Pequea, and their names and descendants are now widely scattered. In 1712 Isaac de Turk settled near Oley in Berks County, and he and his fellow French settlers through their numerous descendants maintained their native language down to quite recent times. The lists of emigrants given in the Pennsylvania Archives contain many names of French families coming to Pennsylvania in 1736 and on for a number of years, from Alsace and Lorraine. Their sons won distinction as soldiers in the War of Independence, and in important civil posts. In Delaware and in Maryland there were numerous French settlers, notably the Bayards. Of the Du Ponts the earliest was a settler on the Santee in South Carolina in 1694. His grand-nephew, Pierre Samuel Du Pont de Nemours, an active Girondist in France, and well known by his writings as an economist and by his activity in public life, followed his sons, who had established industries on the Brandywine that have made them famous.

From this family sprung Admiral Du Pont and General Du Pont and other useful citizens. Among Penn's early settlers were some French, and very good citizens they were. The Doz, De la Val, Du Castle, Reboteau, of the Isle du Rhe, Imbert of Nisme, Le Chevalier of Normandy, Boudinots, Duchés of La Rochelle, Benezet of Montpellier, all are well known. The Cressons were from Picardy, the Garrigues from Montpellier, and the Cassers from Languedoc. The records of Christ Church and of the Lutheran churches of Philadelphia are full of the names of these early French Huguenot settlers and their families. In Germantown were the Le Bruns, De la Plaines, and later the Duvals, Clapiers, and many others, and Duval Street and Clapier Street still perpetuate their old homes. In the Perkiomen and Lower Schuylkill valleys were Boyers, De Frains or De Fresnes, Pechins, Purviances, Tregos, Dubois, La Barres, Le Quais, De la Cours, Bigonets, Loreaux, who became Lorah; Le Char, Leshers; Retteaus, Rettew; Perdeaus, Barto; while in the rich Oley Valley of Berks County were De Turks, Bertolets, De Bonnevilles, De Vaus, De la Planch, now Planks; while nearer Reading settled Dubrees, Boilieus, Tonnelliers, who became Kieffers, and in this as in many other cases the French origin was almost lost. In the upper Delaware and Lehigh country are found De Normandie, Bessonet, Le Valleau, De Pue, now De Pew; Michelet, later Mickle; Jourdan, Santee, from Burgundy; Boileau, Balliet, from Languedoc; while in Lancaster County among the early settlers were French traders, Bezillion, Chartiers, Lebort, Perrines, Mathiots, Le Roys, De Bos, as well as many later comers.

The records of the churches of all the many sects settled in Pennsylvania are full of names showing the French origin of many of the members. The Le Beaus are now Lebos, the Bésores are Bashore and Baysore, according to the county they lived in, Berks or Franklin. In Lebanon the Jacques became Jacobs; in Dauphin, De Saussier became Sausser; Monier from Lorraine, Money; Grosjean, Groshong; and Souplis, Suplee. Across the Susquehanna in York were Perots, who became Berrot; Doutel, Dutill; Votturin of Lorraine, Woodring;

Moreau, Morrow; St. Gris, Sangree; La Mothe, Lamott; and the Cessnas and Piatts are among the descendants of French Huguenot settlers. In Western Pennsylvania are Cassatts (originally Cassart), Bonnetts, Marchands, Leisures, Mestrezats, relatives of Albert Gallatin; Brunot; Dreyvault, now Dravo; Fortineaux, now Fortny; Boucquet became Buckey; Mottier, Motter; and from Pennsylvania through Maryland into Virginia these families are found. Even of the poor Acadian exiles some were left in Pennsylvania, and often their names were changed out of all resemblance to the French originals, just as the Custom House officers wrote the names of immigrants on the lists printed in the Pennsylvania Archives, in a way that makes it very puzzling to identify now. More to be proud of than noble ancestry, are the names of such men as Audubon, Bayard, Benezet, Dupont, Duponceau, Gallaudet, Gallatin, and others of French birth or descent, who have served their country with honor.

An early French settlement on the upper Delaware in Pennsylvania was that of Nicholas Dupuy, in 1725, and a deed for three thousand acres from the Indians in 1727 was confirmed by a patent from the Proprietors, the Penns, and their grantee, William Allen. Another early French settlement in that neighborhood was that of the La Barre, Le Barre, or La Bar family, in 1730. This name is still honorably preserved and distinguished by descendants.

In 1794 François Vannier of St. Domingo bought land in Monroe County, Pennsylvania. In 1816 Constantine Pinchot of Bretielle, France, settled with his son Cyrille on a tract of four hundred acres near Milford, Pike County, Pennsylvania, still known locally as the French lot. His descendants still own the land, and have shown a capital example of the success of French thrift and intelligence. One of the descendants is the head of the Forestry Bureau of the United States, and has by word and deed done an infinite service by his skill and intelligence in the cause of preserving and restoring the wealth of American timber.

Fauchere, Le Clerck, Bournique, Loreaux, are among the names of later French settlers on the upper Delaware, and some of the descendants still live and prosper there. In the western part of Pennsylvania, once a French territory, there are still traces of the early French settlements, both in place names, such as Fort Du Quesne in Pittsburg, and in the names of descendants of those whose nationality was transferred from France to Great Britain and then to the United States.

IV

FRENCH SOLDIERS IN THE UNITED STATES

MANY of the French soldiers who served in the American Revolution returned to France and left more or less interesting memoirs. The Swedish Count Fersen tried to save Marie Antoinette, and in his old age lost his life in an outbreak in Stockholm. The Marquis Armand de la Rouarie, who as Colonel Armand, led a cavalry regiment under Washington, became a noted chief of the loyalists in Brittany, and his romantic story is told with great fulness of detail in recent books. Others became very noted French generals and statesmen. Many of the French officers who served with Rochambeau have left notes of the impression made on them by Washington. " He has," says Fersen, " the air of a hero, his figure fine and majestic, his manner gentle and kindly, his smile agreeable, his welcome simple and dignified." Segur says: " He inspired, rather than commanded, respect;" Lauzun has only praise for his moderation, and Lafayette entrusted his son to him as to a second father. The Rochambeaus, father and son, handed down as heirlooms the portrait of Washington that he had presented, and the guns taken at Yorktown which he gave them as trophies, and the sword he had exchanged with the older soldier. Of the French officers who served in America, Lauzun, Duc de Gontaut Biron, served France in its wars only to end his life on the scaffold. Berthier became Prince of Wagram, Dumas a general under Napoleon.

Chastellux not only served with distinction under Rochambeau, but his " Travels in 1780–82 " furnish the first really trustworthy record of life in the United States, as jotted down by a cultivated European, who had helped them to gain their independence, and thus he rendered a twofold service.

Even " Tom " Paine brought with him to this country his Paris host, Bonneville, and his family, and one of the sons became an officer of distinction in the United States army. Washington Irving wrote an account of Bonne-

5

ville's Western explorations. In doing this he paid tribute to John Jacob Astor, whose purse contributed very largely to the expense of this and other early Western explorations, and even if he did it with a view to later commercial dealings, both gift and motive did him credit. Colonel Bonneville was not the first of the name to do good service in America. An earlier De Bonneville served as an engineer in the old French War in 1763, and published in 1771 a book on America. The younger Bonneville, born in France in 1795, was appointed to West Point, graduated in 1815, and in 1831–3 was engaged in explorations in the Rocky Mountains and California. His journal, edited and amplified by Washington Irving, was published in 1837. He was brevetted for gallantry in the Mexican War, and later for long and faithful services through the Civil War; he was the oldest officer on the retired list at the time of his death. Washington Irving met him at Mr. Astor's, through whose generous help both profited, and Irving edited his manuscript notes, and published his Travels to the Rocky Mountains, in Philadelphia, through Carey,

Lea and Blanchard, in 1837, as in some sort a supplement to his Astoria, in which he gave an account of Astor's unsuccessful efforts to establish trade with Oregon and the then unknown West.

The Comte de Paris and the Prince de Joinville not only showed their earnest sympathy for the Union by brief service in arms for it, but the former made a real contribution to military history by that of the Civil War, and the latter contributed a short account of the Army of the Potomac from actual personal observation. On both sides in the great struggle there were French soldiers, in some cases whole regiments from New York and companies from New Orleans and Louisiana, and all gave a good proof that the old Gallic spirit had endured even in their new homes and in spite of years of peace and harmony.

The Society of the Cincinnati in both the United States and in France keeps alive the memories of the alliance between France and the United States, and the successful issue of the long struggle for independence. But apart from these historic events, there were many

Frenchmen to whom the United States is indebted. L'Enfant laid out the city of Washington in a way that commands to-day the admiration of American architects, and it is by restoring his plans that the National Capital is to take its place among the great cities of the world.

Balch's " The French in America " gives as among the French officers who returned to this country to settle, De la Gardette, of the regiment Soissonais; De Beaulieu, of the Armand Legion, settled at Asylum; Colombe returned to Philadelphia after being imprisoned with Lafayette at Olmütz; Dupetit Thouars, in 1795-96 at Asylum, fell at the Battle of the Nile; Duponceau became a leader of the Philadelphia Bar; Duportail came to the United States in 1794, and died at sea while returning to France in 1804; L'Enfant, architect, who laid out Washington, died in Maryland in 1825.

Vicomte de Noailles [Louis Marie] was born in Paris in 1756, second son of the Marshal de Noailles, married his cousin Louise, daughter of the Duc de Noailles, and granddaughter of D'Aguessau. He was young, handsome, ambitious of glory, a patriot. Returning to the United States, he was active in forwarding, with Dupetit Thouars, the colony of Asylum in Pennsylvania. Returning to active service, he was wounded in a successful naval engagement, and died in Havana January 3, 1804. His grandson was one of the French descendants of the French who served in the American Revolution, to visit this country on the Centenary of Yorktown.

Major L'Enfant, author of the plan of the City of Washington, D. C., has been properly described as a neglected genius. Fortunately the wheel of fortune has recently turned in his favor, and the great architects of our own day have paid tribute to his memory by adopting his plans as the basis for the improvements now under way, to make Washington a metropolis worthy of the nation and suitable for its capital. Born in Paris in 1754, he came to America in 1777, with Du Coudray, the French engineer, served as a volunteer, was commissioned a captain of engineers in the United States army, was attached to the light infantry in the Army of the South, led the advance in the assault on Savannah under Lincoln, and was wounded at the head of his force; was made prisoner at the siege of Charleston, South Carolina, and later was exchanged for Captain v. Heyden of the Anspach Yägers, and served as engineer under Washington. He received a pension from the King of France and a brevet as major from Congress. He remodelled the City Hall in New York for the use of Congress, and in acknowledgment received the thanks of the corporation, the freedom of the city, and a grant of ten acres of city land, which he declined. In 1789 he wrote to Washington of the importance of a plan for the city of Washington worthy of the nation, and of the protection of the seacoast as a matter of national importance. He was appointed to prepare the plans for the city of Washington, and although for many years their execution was postponed and marred by the interference of less competent hands, they have recently been revived and are now being used, with due recognition, as the basis for a great and beautiful metropolitan capital. He died in 1825 in Prince

George's County, Maryland, just beyond the line of the District of Columbia. To his architectural genius and engineering skill the United States owe the plan submitted by L'Enfant in 1791, and adopted by Congress and approved by Washington, and with its execution now his fame will be perpetuated in the city of Washington.

In October, 1778, D'Estaing issued in the name of Louis XVI a proclamation to all the "old French" in North America, inviting them to escape the tyranny of Great Britain and join the French forces in their help to secure liberty for all Americans.

The French officers by turns paid their respect to Washington. Chastellux, Noailles, Damas, and others were presented by Lafayette with Laval, Custine, the Deux Ponts brothers, Charlus, Saint Maime, La Corbière, and Washington received them with great heartiness, and spoke to and of them in high praise—called Duplessis his old acquaintance.

The Vicomte de Noailles in his "Marins et Soldats Français en Amérique pendant la Guerre de l'Indépendance des Etats Unis, 1778–

1783 " (Paris, 1903), emphasizes the hearty welcome given to the French army in Philadelphia on its way to Yorktown, and later the unity between the French engineers in that force and those in the American army, in their operations that helped so greatly to the surrender of Cornwallis. Du Portail, Du Gouvion, and Rochefontaine were engineers in the army under Washington.

He also gives a letter written about Luzerne, the French Minister to the United States, by Rochambeau, saying that it was lucky Luzerne had joined him, for his house in Philadelphia was struck by lightning, his bed, etc., destroyed by it, and an artillery officer left there on account of illness, killed,—" a great argument in favor of Mr. Franklin's Conductors, the owner of the house occupied by Luzerne never permitting one to be put up, as he was opposed to Franklin's plan."

D'Autichamp, who was made a brigadier for his services at Yorktown, was no doubt the one who later joined in the French colony at Asylum, Pennsylvania. Noailles mentions among the French officers of the American war,

De Laumoy, who served as colonel of engineers in the American army, was in Martinique as second in command in 1789–91, and came to Philadelphia as an exile, remaining there until 1803; returned to France and was put on the retired list in 1811, and died in Paris in 1832.

Many of the French officers procured employment in the United States. Toussard and Bernard in the army, L'Enfant as architect and engineer, and others in civil life. One of the most ambitious efforts was that made by Quesnay de Beaurepaire, to found an international Academy of Sciences and Letters, in Richmond, Virginia. It is fully described by Professor Herbert B. Adams as follows: [1]

" The United States Academy, at Richmond, a survival of French influence, was a very remarkable attempt made in the latter part of the Eighteenth Century to establish the higher education in this country upon a

---

[1] Herbert B. Adams: Thomas Jefferson and the University of Virginia (United States Bureau of Education, Circular of Information No. 1, 1888).

grand scale. It was an attempt, growing out of the French alliance with the United States, to plant in Richmond, the new capital of Virginia, a kind of French Academy of the Arts and Sciences, with branch academies in Baltimore, Philadelphia, and New York. The institution was to be at once national and international. It was to be affiliated with the royal societies of London, Paris, and Brussels, and with other learned bodies in Europe. It was to be composed of a president, vice-president, six counsellors, a treasurer-general, a secretary, a recorder, an agent for taking European subscriptions, French professors, masters, artists in chief attached to the academy, twenty-five resident and one hundred and seventy-five non-resident associates, selected from the best talent of the Old World and the New. The Academy proposed to publish yearly from its own press in Paris an annual report, to communicate to France and other countries in Europe a knowledge of the natural products of North America, and to send specimens of its flora and fauna abroad. Experts from Paris were to be the teachers. The projector was the Chevalier

Quesnay de Beaurepaire, grandson of the great economist, Quesnay. He came to this country to aid in the Revolution, and served as captain in Virginia in 1777–78; he raised sixty thousand francs and had one hundred subscribers. Their names were printed in a pamphlet issued in Paris in 1788, showing that he had support in Baltimore, Philadelphia, Trenton, Elizabeth, Newark, and New York, and from Steuben and other worthies. Franklin's daughter, Mrs. Bache, wrote to him asking his support to this scheme ' for the education of young men after they have graduated from college.' The cornerstone was laid in Richmond June 24, 1786, in the presence of local authorities and of a number of French supporters — Raguet, Audrin, La Case, Omphery, Noel, Dossière, Bartholomy, Cureau, and Duval. He returned to Paris, secured a favorable report of a commission of the Academy of Science consisting of La Lande, Thouin, and Lavoisier, certified by Condorcet, and of the Academy of Painting, signed by Vernet and others. He enlisted the interest of Beaumarchais, La Fayette, Houdon, Malesherbes, Lavoisier, Luzerne,

Montalembert, and Rochefoucauld in Paris, and in London of Bancroft, Paine, Dr. Richard Price, Jonathan Trumbull, Rutledge, Benjamin West, and Jefferson. Quesnay's plan included schools for foreign languages, mathematics, design, architecture, painting, sculpture, engraving, physics, astronomy, geography, chemistry, mineralogy, botany, anatomy and natural history. The building was completed, and later became a theatre, and was used for the meeting of the Virginia Convention which, in 1788, ratified the Constitution of the United States. One professor was appointed, Dr. John Rouelle, to be mineralogist-in-chief and Professor of Natural History, Chemistry, and Botany, but it is doubtful if he ever came to this country. The French Revolution put a stop to the plan, and all that is known of it is from the rare copies of Quesnay's Memoir."

"A French Volunteer in the War of Independence" is the story of the Chevalier de Pontgibaud (translated by R. B. Douglass, published by Carrington, Paris, 1897). He was one of the many French soldiers who had served under Rochambeau, and in his three visits to this country had abundant opportunity to contrast the people and the country. He speaks of the colony at Asylum in Pennsylvania, founded mainly by De Noailles, for both in France and in the United States it attracted much attention, and the story of the emigrant settlers, and their hardships, was the subject of a great deal of discussion. He says that in 1793 six hundred French refugees from St. Domingo arrived in Philadelphia at the time of a severe outbreak of yellow fever. The French Patriotic Society contributed eight hundred dollars and a fund of eleven thousand dollars was raised for their relief. He mentions, too, the arrival in 1798 of a large number of French refugees with many negroes from Port au Prince in Philadelphia, and the effort of General Toussard, then in command of Fort Mifflin, near the city, to relieve their distress. Later on he reports that eight vessels brought two hundred and twenty-seven French refugees.

V

EARLY FRENCH TRAVELLERS IN THE UNITED STATES

CHATEAUBRIAND came to the United States in 1791 with a letter to Washington from the Marquis de la Rouarie, who as Colonel Armand had borne a creditable part in the American War of Independence. At that time there was an increasing emigration from France to escape the growing violence of the French Revolution. On the shores of the Ohio an asylum was opened in the land of liberty to those who fled from its excesses. Landing in Baltimore, he went to Philadelphia, where he found many exiles from France and St. Domingo. Chateaubriand, in republication of his works in his old age, notes the French place names, dwelt on the county of Bourbon with its county-seat Paris, in Kentucky, and the town of Versailles in that State, and the county of Marengo in Alabama. He quotes Père du

Creux, a Jesuit writer, as authority for the fact that a French colony was established in Onondaga, New York, in 1655, and Charlevoix as mentioning that the missionaries sent there in 1654 established a French colony in 1658, which was abandoned in 1668,—but these are both doubtful.

Chateaubriand spent only a few months in the United States, but he drew from earlier writers, such as the Abbé Raynal, and from earlier travellers, Bartram and others, much of the material for his novels, poems, historical essays, etc. His stay in Baltimore, Philadelphia, New York, and Albany, seems to have left little trace among their usually hospitable citizens. In Baltimore the Sulpicians have a tradition from one of their order who was his fellow passenger from France, that Chateaubriand tried to convert some of his young men to the liberalism then fashionable. In Philadelphia he presented his letter from Colonel Armand, of the American Army, but later known as Marquis de la Rouarie, leader of the Bretons in their counter-revolution for the Royalists, and after some delay, owing to

Washington's absence in the South, was received. He says that Washington was very incredulous as to the discovery of a northwest passage, the ostensible object of his visit to America, but Chateaubriand said: " It is an easier task than to create a nation, and that you have done." Washington invited him to dinner and he accepted. He compares Washington and Bonaparte, much to the advantage of the great American, who left the United States as the trophy won by him in battle, while Bonaparte deprived his country of liberty and betrayed it, and dying left a name without blessing. " Washington," he writes, " was the representative of the needs, the ideas, the intelligence, the opinions of his time; he advanced the movement of its best intellects; he sacrificed everything for his country; his glory is the common patrimony of growing civilization, his fame a sanctuary whence flow endless blessings for the world."

Chateaubriand had seen both Washington and Bonaparte, and as he suffered at the hands of the latter for his opposition, was naturally inclined to find in Washington a much purer, better and higher type of heroism. Much of his recollection of his short journey in the United States is in his Historical Essays. He made a pilgrimage to Lexington, the first battle-ground of the American Revolution, and he describes his visit to Niagara with more poetry than fact. On his way from Albany through the solitary forests, he found a Frenchman, once cook for Rochambeau, teaching the savage Indians to dance—they half naked, with rings in their noses, feathers in their hair; he powdered, in full dress, fiddle in hand, and taking his pay in poultry and bear meat. What he saw of Niagara is described in his novel, Atala, but his Travels to the South are largely drawn from Bartram's and other books. Returned to Philadelphia, he heard of the execution of the king, and at once returned to France and then to England, where he began the long series of books on American subjects that gave him fame.

More of a poet and a romancer than a serious statesman or a man of letters, he has said little that shows how he was impressed by his short stay in America. He was in

Baltimore and Philadelphia at a time when many of his countrymen found refuge there, but he seems to have been but little with them. His companions on his travels were Hollanders, representatives of the large land-owners of that country. While the Philosophical Society and the Binghams in Philadelphia were opening their doors to the French exiles of all political opinions—Noailles, Omer Talon, Talleyrand, Volney, Brissot de Warville, Moreau, and many others are of record in one way or another—there is no mention of Chateaubriand, whose fame was to exceed that of all our other French visitors.

" A Sketch of the United States from 1800 to 1810," by Chevalier Felix de Beaujour, at one time consul general of France in the United States, was not allowed to be published in France, on the score of its favorable tone towards Great Britain, but in 1814 a translation was published in London, with notes, etc., by William Walton. The editor said the author's aim was to take from Great Britain its trade with the United States, and the notes· are intended to correct his hostility to the

IN THE UNITED STATES

English system of trade, so soon to lead to war with the United States.

General Victor Collot had served with Rochambeau in the American War of Independence, later became governor of Guadeloupe, until its capture by the English, then came to Philadelphia, and with his adjutant, Warin, by authority of Adet, the French Minister to the United States, under an order dated " Phila. 24th ventose, 4th Year of the Republic One and Indivisible," made a long tour through North America, of which the account was not published until 1826, long after the death of the travellers.

Collot speaks of the few memorials of Jesuits or other missionaries, written " more than sixty years since " (his own journey began in 1796), as the only monuments which France can produce of its labors and researches in North America. His journey took him through Pennsylvania to the Monongahela and Ohio. Pittsburg he found a town of one hundred and fifty houses. Thence he started in his own boat, purchased at McKeesport, with two Canadians and three Americans, for New

Orleans, and he gives a minute record of his daily observations. In Marietta he found a few French families, unfortunate victims of American land speculation on the part of the Scioto Company. He blames the French for their folly in trying to establish a colony without using the least precaution to safeguard their ownership, but he condemns unqualifiedly the managers who abandoned the poor settlers. At Gallipolis there was a population reckoned at ninety to ninety-five men, and forty to forty-five women, the wreck of the Scioto community. Congress granted seven acres to each family, not sufficient for their maintenance, and therefore they were extremely miserable; the site unhealthy, the land bad, the houses small log huts, flanked by three block-houses, the whole palisaded with great picquets, the place dirty and the abode of wretchedness. Congress, in 1796, voted each family two hundred and fifty acres of land near the Little Scioto, as indemnity for the suffering, robbery, and murder of which they had been the victims, through the carelessness, perfidy, and knavery of the agents of the Land Company which had brought them here.

At Louisville he found a suburb laid out by a French settler; at St. Vincent's, a small village of one hundred families, the greater part French, ruined by General Clark during the last war, as were also the settlements in Illinois. Another small French establishment was Onia or Oniatenon, a trading point for furs. On the Mississippi there were French settlements on both banks of the river. At St. Louis the two hundred French were excellent patriots, all devoted to France, laborers in easy circumstances, and prosperous merchants, and in other places near at hand were considerable settlements of French.

VI

FRENCH EXILES IN THE UNITED STATES

THE records of the Roman Catholic Church form an important share in the historical collections of that body.

The American Catholic Historical Society has printed in its Proceedings, the registers of the churches in Philadelphia, St. Mary's and St. Joseph's; in them are the births, marriages, and deaths of many French families, refugees from St. Domingo and other West Indian French colonies at their sanguinary revolutions. Father Cibot, who made some of these entries, was himself one of the exiles from St. Domingo. Among the names on these registers are those of De Serres, Drouillard, Langlade, Gobert, Balestrier, St. Didier, Petit, Bauduy, Roseau, Des Cloches, Chaudron, De la Lande-Ormund (in this case the husband came from Brittany, the wife from Pondicherry). This colony of French exiles was long one of the characteristic features of Philadelphia. Gathered together on Front Street and out Spruce and Pine as far as Eighth Street, there were the homes of merchants, doctors, lawyers, and men of letters.

For years the schools kept by Frenchmen and women,—Picots, Guillous, Segoignes, Bolmars, Grellots—were the best in the country. In 1793 the French Benevolent Society was organized, and on its list of members were the names of De l'Isle, Duval, Clapier, Laval, Bujac, De la Roche, Gardette, Droz, Brugiere, Monges, Garesché, Dabadie, Maillard, Pintard, Crousillat, Rodrigues, Dutilh, Deschapelles, Mazurie, Breuil, Prevost, Besson, Belin, Troubat, Rousseau, Mathieu, Salignac, Laussatt, and later on such names as Duponceau, Girard, Thouron, Turreau, Rozet, Vauclain, Laval, Vanuxem. From that day to this the list attests the presence in Philadelphia of French families proud of the history of this useful organization and still continuing its useful and modest career of benevolence. A sad record of these exiles is found in the monuments in St. Mary's Roman Catholic graveyard, to the

Melizets, the Laussats, the Lejambres, the Bouviers, the Bories, the Keatings, the Tessières, and others.

In "Reminiscences of Wilmington, Delaware" by E. Montgomery, (Philadelphia, 1851), there is mention of many French exiles settled there; M. Martel, the tutor of Aaron Burr's daughter, and Dr. Bayard and Dr. Capelle, who had served under Lafayette in the Revolution; I. Isambrie, a soldier under Napoleon until his return from Egypt, with his wife, a native of St. Domingo,—he took Marshal Grouchy and General Moreau out on shooting excursions; Ferdin and Baudry; la Marquise de Sourci; Dr. Didie, the Gareschéramily, Peter Provenchere, a tutor of the Duc de Berri, and his relative the wife of John Keating of Philadelphia; Mrs. Capron, who kept a successful school; M. Bergerac, a teacher, later a professor in St. Mary's College, Baltimore; M. Sarsney; and with these exiles, came many colored people, who were respected for good qualities. Thus in Wilmington, Delaware, too, the later French exiles found shelter, and many of them employment with the Du-ponts and Gareschés and Lammots in their large and important industries. Among the French settlers in Philadelphia was John Bouvier, who came in 1802, at fifteen years of age, with his family, from the south of France. Quakers, they were warmly welcomed; the father died of yellow fever, the son became a printer and later a lawyer, and is well known by his " Institutes," his Law Dictionary and other works.

As early as 1803 a colony of French Trappists arrived in Baltimore, and soon made a home in Adams County, Pennsylvania; thence going to near Louisville, and making settlements in Kentucky. Among the Roman Catholic clergy were many Frenchmen, among them Archbishop Cheverus of Bordeaux, who was for many years Bishop of Boston, Massachusetts. He kept in touch with his old parishioners down to the end of his long and honored life, and he was but one of many French priests in the United States.

Among the noteworthy early French priests was the Rev. Louis Barth de Walbach, of Alsace. Born at Munster in 1764, he arrived in

Baltimore in 1791, and after long years of active service in the ministry of his church, he and his brother, General John de Walbach, a veteran of the American War of Independence, quietly lived in Georgetown College, District of Columbia, where the former died in 1844, the latter in Baltimore, in 1857.

VII

French Settlers and Exiles in South Carolina [1]

THE Huguenot emigrants, who arrived in Charleston, South Carolina, 1680–86, began their French Church about 1687 on land given by Ralph Izard; Isaac Mazyck, one of the earliest and wealthiest of his race, gave generously to its erection and support.

The prosperity of the Huguenots aroused the jealousy of their neighbors; many of the refugees being possessed of considerable property in France, had sold it and brought the money to England. Having purchased large tracts of land with this money, they settled in more advantageous circumstances than the poorer sort of the English emigrants. Having clergymen of their own persuasion, for whom they entertained the highest respect and

[1] "Charleston: The Place and the People," by Mrs. St. Julien Ravenel. New York. Macmillan, 1906.

admiration, they were disposed to encourage them as far as their narrow circumstances would permit. The two pastors who accompanied them were the Reverend Elias Prioleau, of the Church of Pons in Saintonge, whose grandfather, a member of the ducal house of Priuli, had surrendered rank and fortune for the Protestant faith sixty years before; and the Reverend Florente Philippe Trouillard. Prioleau was dead (his monument may be seen in the French Protestant Church of Charleston), but M. Trouillard and his " ancien " or elder, M. Boutelle, petitioned the Proprietors on the injustice done to their people. The Proprietors in answer, ordered that the French have equal justice with Englishmen and enjoy the same privileges. In 1697 an act was passed making aliens free of this part of the province and granting liberty of conscience to all Protestants, with a preamble acknowledging their loyalty and industry. When in 1706 the Huguenots outside of the town cast in their lot with the Episcopal Church, those of Charleston, having a church with ample endowments, kept and preserve to this day their own independent

organization. In 1736 the Huguenots established in a small way the South Carolina Club,
still in active life, which besides assisting in-
digent widows and orphans, established a school
for boys and girls.

In the Revolutionary War, the Huguenots
furnished such soldiers as Motte, grandson of
the first immigrant of that name; Marion,
Huger, Robert, and many others. In 1792
the French refugees from St. Domingo found
shelter in New Orleans and Charleston, where
they were received with kindness and sympathy.
The townsfolk threw open their houses to receive the fugitives. Nothing could exceed their
courage and cheerfulness. Uncomplaining,
gay, and pathetically grateful, they won the
esteem and respect of their hosts. No one had
cause to repent his hospitality. For their
assistance the city gave $12,500, besides the
proceeds of a concert and many gifts, and the
United States government appropriated $1750.
This help enabled many of them to begin some
occupation; they would take no more than was
absolutely necessary, and quickly bestirred
themselves for their own support. They were

accomplished in music, painting, and the languages, and pupils were soon found. Some of the gentlemen were good musicians and entered the orchestra of the theatre, which greatly benefited by their skill. Thirteen of the best teachers in town were refugees. Two of the schools established by them were long the most fashionable. In an inferior class, the best bakers, pastrycooks, dressmakers, hairdressers, and clearstarchers, were refugees or their children, and they were the best dancing-teachers, too. A few who had some knowledge of business became successful merchants, and more than one was distinguished in medicine. One of these, Dr. Polony, was the most eminent, being a member of learned European societies and a correspondent of Buffon. Seven years after their arrival, the Duc de la Rochefoucauld Liancourt visited Charleston, and in his Travels speaks warmly of the gentleness, courtesy and agreeability of these refugees, and the untiring kindness and liberality of the citizens, who were well rewarded by the example of good manners and accomplishments which embellished society. The mother of Joseph Jefferson was one of

these refugees, and the great actor told the
story of her life and its many vicissitudes in
his autobiography.

In the churchyard of the Roman Catholic
Church are many graves of St. Domingan
refugees, among them those of the daughters
of Count de Grasse, the commander of the
French auxiliary fleet during the Revolution.

In 1825 Lafayette visited Charleston, and
was greeted by Colonel Huger, who had risked
his life in a vain effort to rescue him from
prison. He renewed his acquaintance with the
survivors of his campaigns in the Revolution,
with General Pinckney, and the daughter of
General Greene, and the widow of Colonel
Washington. Later his nephew De Lasteyrie
visited Charleston and married a Charleston
girl, Lafayette Seabrook, named in honor of
his uncle's visit to her parents in 1825. In
the midst of the excitement of nullification in
1833, a subscription ball was given under the
patronage of Count de Choiseul, for " poor old
M. Fayolle, who had lost his all in a ship-
wreck," an old St. Domingan refugee, who had
taught half Charleston to dance. Choiseul was

for many years French consul at Charleston; a royalist, his eldest son fell fighting gallantly as captain of the Louisiana Zouaves in the Civil War, and the second son became Marquis de Choiseul.

VIII

French Settlements in the West and in Canada

"Origine et Progrès de la Mission du Kentucky" (Paris, 1821), is a pamphlet giving an encouraging account of the French settled in that State. Twenty-four Catholic families came to Kentucky in 1785 from Maryland; their number increased, and in 1793 Bishop Carroll of Baltimore sent M. Badin, of Orleans, who for many years had spiritual charge of the Catholics in Kentucky, while M. Rivet of Limoges came in 1795 as vicar general to Vincennes, on the Wabash, in Indiana. In 1797 and 1799 Messrs. Fournier and Salmon of Blois, followed by a number of French priests exiled from France by the Revolution, came to Kentucky. M. Olivier of Nantes settled at Prairie du Rocher, Illinois, and served there and at Kaskaskia, Cahokia, Saint Louis, Ste. Genevieve, etc. In 1808 an episcopate was

7

97

established at Bardstown, Kentucky, where later French Trappists established a convent with a branch at Cahokia, in which many Indians were educated. At Gallipolis, in Ohio, where in 1791 there was a colony of French people, victims of a miserable speculation, who had mostly abandoned the place, Messrs. Barrières and Badin baptized forty children in 1793, and the whole village was inspired by the service.

The popularity of the French is attested by the names, Bourbon County and Paris, Versailles, Louisville, in Kentucky. There were five Frenchmen bishops,—M. Marechal of Orleans, in Baltimore; M. Cheverus of Paris, in Boston; M. Flaget of Auvergne, in Kentucky; M. David of Nantes, his coadjutor; M. Dubourg of St. Louis, Bishop of Louisiana and Florida. M. Flaget came to America in 1792 with Messrs. David and Badin. At Bardstown many important schools were under the care of French priests. An appeal was made to the people of France to help them with money, books, church ornaments, etc. It would be interesting to know how far it was answered.

Drovine's " Les Royalistes Français réfugiés au Canada " (Quebec, 1905), gives many facts of interest. In 1793 Abbé Desjardins recalled from Gallipolis Dom Didier, a Benedictine, from the Abbey of St. Denis. He says: Gallipolis was founded in 1790 on the banks of the Ohio. In 1796 the colony numbered about eighty, and in 1805 this was reduced to twenty. Asylum, on the Susquehanna, was founded in 1794 by Messrs. Noailles and Talon; it began with thirty houses, and included among its number, M. Blacons, deputy to the constituent assembly; Bec de Lièvre, canon; Archdeacon Toul; Abbé Fromentin, Abbé Charles, M. d'Andelot of the French infantry; Du Petit Thouars, officer of the navy; Brevost of Paris; Mme. d'Autrepont. These settlers became farmers and made potash, sugar, molasses, and vinegar. Many priests came to Canada, and Drovine tells their story with great fulness and detail. The same ship that brought Chateaubriand to Baltimore carried five priests and two seminarists. After a voyage of three months they landed and soon established a seminary near Baltimore, in 1791; later, in 1792, eight more arrived, and in 1793-4-5-6-8, new arrivals came, in all twenty-nine, while forty-five went to Canada. Of the former six became bishops, one an Archbishop and Cardinal, Cheverus of Boston, later of Bordeaux. While the clergy were helped by large subscriptions and by the government, an effort was made to quicken the emigration of lay royalists to Canada. Chateaubriand says that in London some sold coal, others made hats, some taught French. Then it was " a proposal for a subscription to form Colonies in Canada of French Emigrants, Royalists, and ecclesiastics " was published in London, and its execution was undertaken by Count Joseph de Puisaye, who had been a soldier by turns in the Cent Suisses, in the National Guard, in the Federal Army, at the head of the Chouans in Brittany, where he organized a Military Council and issued three millions of paper money like the assignats of the Republic. He went to London and enlisted the help of Pitt, who gave him a command in the unsuccessful attack on Quiberon, which was repelled by Hoche. Thiers says he had great intelligence, a rare talent for organization, activity of mind and body, and vast ambition. He wrote a paper on the establishment of a French colony in Canada, and five hundred persons applied to join—eight marquises, two bishops, one Benedictine monk, two priests, one doctor, six counts, one baron, many naval officers, seven Chevaliers de St. Louis, a princess, a countess, a marquise and a long list of other noble personages. Out of thirty-eight who actually emigrated few of the people of rank really left England. Arrived in Canada in October, 1798, Puisaye, strongly recommended by the home authorities, was allowed five thousand acres, and land was set apart on and near Lake Ontario for the settlers and a town and farms. Puisaye was made a justice of the peace and commandant of a corps with one major commanding, two captains, two lieutenants, four sub-lieutenants, one adjutant, one quartermaster, one chaplain, one surgeon and an assistant, six sergeants, eight corporals, and one hundred and fifty soldiers. The land, over four thousand acres, was distributed among the settlers, but of the forty, only twenty-five remained. Puisaye himself soon went back to England, and others followed, so that the colony was practically abandoned. Later a mysterious person settled near Trois Rivières, who it is supposed was the Duc de Vicence, Caulaincourt, one of Napoleon's generals; he came in 1816 and left in 1820, but the mystery of his identity was never really solved. Most of the clergymen remained and many were useful parish priests, some teachers, others high dignitaries of their church.

IX

Brillat Savarin in the United States

Brillat Savarin came as an exile from the French Revolution in 1793, and resided three years in New York, where he taught French and played in the orchestra of a theatre, returning to France in 1796, where he filled important posts, and died in 1826.

In his " Physiologie du Goût " he says that in Boston he found Julien keeping a restaurant—he had been cook for the Archbishop of Bordeaux; Brillat Savarin showed him how to cook eggs with cheese, and it was so popular that Julien sent him in New York part of a young roe deer from Canada. Captain Collet made quite a fortune in selling ices and sorbets in New York in 1794–95. In New York he met the Vcte. de Massue and M. Fehr of Marseilles, exiles, too. In Connecticut he dined at a farm house near Hartford (in October, 1794), on corned beef, stewed goose, a haunch of mutton, vegetables in plenty, and two huge foaming pots of excellent cider, and later excellent tea. They shot next day partridges, squirrels, and wild turkeys; then returned to supper, ate like famished men, with an ample bowl of punch to crown the entertainment. His host, M. Barlow, had served in the War of Independence, and spoke in high praise of " the Marquis " La Fayette. The daughter sang " Yankee Doodle," " Major André's Lament," and other popular songs. His host said in bidding him adieu, that he was a happy man—he owned his property, his daughters knit his stockings, his shoes and clothes were made from his own flocks, which provided his food, too; he had no locks on his doors, taxes were nominal, Congress favors our rising industry, agents visit us to purchase what we have to sell—*e. g.*, flour at $24 per ton [*sic*], the usual price having been $8. The sound of the drum is never heard except on the Fourth of July, and only on that day soldiers are seen.

During his ride home, Savarin was thinking how to cook his turkey, and he gave a dinner at Hartford to his American friends, with the wings of the partridges "en papillote," the gray squirrels stewed in Madeira, while the roast turkey was pleasing to the eye, flattering to the smell and delicious to the taste; and when the last particle had vanished, there was a universal murmur of applause.

His friend shot wild turkeys in Carolina and found them excellent, of much better flavor than those reared in Europe. Savarin, who was a cousin of Mme. Récamier, always spoke with pleasure of his stay in the United States.

X

FRENCH LAND COMPANIES IN THE UNITED STATES

GOUVERNEUR MORRIS was busy with land sales abroad, as well as with diplomatic missions, and to his great friends, for he was as rich in them as in American lands, he was constantly pointing out the great future for investment in them. In 1794 he notes that Le Ray de Chaumont had been ahead of him in dealing with the Baron de Coppet, Necker. Already in 1789 he had broached to his friends in France a plan for a settlement on the banks of the river St. Lawrence for those who want to go out to America. In 1790 he writes to Robert Morris that frequent applications were made to him for advice about American lands, but he felt that it would hardly do for him to bear the responsibility of advising French citizens to abandon their native country. He was therefore anxious that an office should be opened in Paris where maps could be seen and titles lodged, adding: " Purchasers here are for the most part ignorant of geography. So far from thinking the forests a disadvantage, they are captivated with the idea of having their chateaux surrounded by magnificent trees. They naturally expect superb highways over the pathless deserts, and see with the mind's eye numerous barges in every stream." His journey in 1794 to Quebec and Northern New York only increased his faith in the great future of the then " West," and he described his lands there as the finest he ever saw. In 1808 he wrote to Mme. de Staël: " I shall expect to see you with your son next spring. I know your friend Le Ray keeps you well informed about your affairs. If your landed property were all lying together it would be more valuable, because it could be managed with more ease and less expense." Indeed at thirty-five, Mme. de Staël was seriously considering Morris' urgent recommendation to go to the United States as a safe refuge from the troubles in Europe. Alike in Paris and in Germany, Morris encouraged his friends of all ranks to save their money by putting it into American land, and no doubt Le Ray de Chaumont and others who planned French colonies in the United States did so with his help.

The elder Le Ray de Chaumont was owner of a luxurious home at Passy, where in one of its dependencies, the Hôtel Valentinois, Franklin found a quiet retreat. Le Ray was Grand Master of the Waters and Forests of France and Honorary Intendant of the Invalides. He was rich and occupied the chateau of Chaumont on the Loire, as well as the house at Passy. He was the close friend of the Duc de Choiseul, his neighbor at Chaumont, and had declined his invitation to enter the ministry, as he preferred to act as an intermediary between the [American] Commissioners and Versailles.[1]

J. Donatien Le Ray de Chaumont was the son of Franklin's host at Passy. The father had advanced large sums to the struggling colonies, and the son came over to settle his father's accounts. At the suggestion of Gouverneur Morris he bought large tracts of

[1] Smyth: Life of Franklin, p. 306.

108

land in Northern New York, and at one time owned thirty thousand acres in Franklin County; seventy-three thousand acres in St. Lawrence County; one hundred and forty-three thousand five hundred acres in Jefferson County; one hundred thousand acres in Lewis County. In 1815, through Duponceau as agent, he conveyed one hundred and fifty thousand acres to Joseph Bonaparte. The actual sale, it is said, was made in France, as Joseph was flying from the allies, and he paid down in gold and precious stones from the store he was carrying off. Joseph was supposed to intend to make a refuge for Napoleon, if he should escape to the United States. It was intended to found large manufacturing establishments on the Black River, to injure the English industries. The details were discussed with a son of Murat, when he was visiting Le Ray in his new home. Le Ray built a large house at Le Rayville, ten miles east of Watertown, and there he entertained many notable French visitors. Joseph Bonaparte came in 1815, and in 1828 built a hunting-lodge, where he spent several summers. Tradition reported in county histories (see Sylvester's "Northern New York," Troy, 1877, and Hough's "Jefferson County," Albany, 1854) that dressed in a green hunting-suit he drove in a coach and six over roads he had cut through the forests, and that on the Black River he had a six-oared gondola. In 1835 he sold his land to John La Farge, of New York. Le Ray began settlements in 1801 and in 1803 laid out the village still called Chaumont. An earlier effort to establish a French colony in the wilds of New York was made by French agents of William Constable, the partner of Macomb, the owner of over three and a half million acres. Their company was to set apart two thousand acres for a city, two thousand acres for a town on Lake Ontario, six thousand acres for artisans, twenty thousand acres for roads, bridges, etc. Le Ray's purchases included part of this vast estate, and his plans are described in the Appendix to St. John de Crévecœur's "Travels in Pennsylvania" (French ed., Paris, 1801). Le Ray sold tracts to many noted Frenchmen, among them Caulaincourt, Real, Grouchy, and De

Furneaux, and it is said that among the purchasers were Mme. de Staël; but at all events Le Ray spent years in promoting settlements on his lands. His last visit to them was made in 1836, and he died in Paris in 1840.

Donatien Le Ray de Chaumont married a Miss Coxe of New Jersey. Their son, Vincent Le Ray de Chaumont, published in Paris, in 1833, a pamphlet, " Renseignemens sur la Partie des Etats Unis la plus favorable aux Agriculteurs venant d'Europe," in which he advises intending French emigrants. He " recommends them to buy and settle on his tract of three hundred thousand acres in Jefferson County, New York, or in the neighborhood, for the State of New York sold its lands much lower than the United States in order to increase its population and its representation and influence in Congress. It is near sawmills, flourmills, etc., and farm products bring much better prices than on the Ohio or anywhere in the West. The country is favorable for vineyards and silk culture. The father and the son are ready to answer any inquiries made of them at their house in Paris." An extract from an address by Major Curry before the Jefferson County Agricultural Society, gives an account of the success of the vines and mulberry trees sent by Le Ray. A circular signed by thirty or more residents of Rosière, the name of the first settlement, commends it and the adjoining lands of M. Le Ray de Chaumont. The signers give their French homes, Haute Saone, Vitrey, Arbecey, Combeaufontaine, etc., and their statement as to the advantages of their new home is attested by the curate, by the bishop of New York, who had himself visited the new colony, and by the French consul general.

In Smyth's Franklin, vol. ix, p. 636, etc., Franklin writes to Le Veillard, of the visit of Messrs. Picque and Saugrain, the latter a brother-in-law of Dr. Guillotin, who had resolved to remove to America, and these two went ahead to investigate the country. Franklin wrote to Guillotin from Philadelphia on May 4, 1788, of bad news of an accident to them on their way down the Ohio, and again on October 23, 1788, confirming the loss of " poor M. Pique " in a wilderness country, and Guillotin never came.

The following books on French colonies in the United States are of interest: "Le Nouveau Mississippi ou les Dangers d'habiter les Bords du Scioto par un patriote Voyageur" [Sergeant Major Roux], Paris, 1790, was written to disabuse the unhappy victims of the Scioto speculators. There was established in Paris, rue Neuve des Petits Champs, No. 162, a company under the name of Scioto. Roux, secretary of the government of Compiegne, who travelled in 1784 through the country of the Scioto and the Ohio, said "he could have bought for twenty-five louis, three or four leagues on the shores of the Ohio, with Congress paper money at ninety per cent., but it would have been a total loss. He warns others that they will lose their money and be worse than slaves. He cites a memoir deposited in the Bureau of the Navy in 1784. He warns his countrymen against the enterprise of the Scioto Company. The soil has little depth, crops diminish yearly, trees have shallow roots, in three years the land must be abandoned. The American works but two or three days a week, that he may drink or idle the others;

the labor is done by ' redemptionists,' men who pay for their passage by hiring themselves out. All men of talent in America are traders. Manufactures can never compete with the superior products of Europe. The Scioto Society boast of the soil, but say nothing of the dangers of climate, want of good water, of the savages, which will destroy any French settlement."

" Lettres écrites des rives de l'Ohio, par Claude François Adrien de Lezay [Marquis de] Marnezia, citoyen de Pensylvanie. Au Fort Pitt et à Paris, an IX de la République." Querard says this pamphlet was seized by the police and is very rare. First letter from " Marieta," [sic] November 15, 1790: " Living in the finest house here, surrounded by generals, majors, colonels, chevaliers of the Order of the Cincinnati,—that is, lodged in a wretched hut, with titled neighbors who drive their own teams, cultivate and very badly their fields, wear poor clothes, entertaining some visiting Indians, who prefer Frenchmen to Americans, since the latter can never cultivate the arts." Second letter, Fort Pitt, No-

vember 2, 1791 [to Bernardin de St. Pierre]:
" I came to America to find a safe and peaceful
retreat from the turmoil of France, to take
possession of a tract of land on the banks of
the Ohio, but I found the promises of the
prospectus of the Scioto Company false in
every respect, except as to the good soil. That
Company has utterly failed in its plans. Leaving New York for my land on the Scioto and
Ohio, I stopped first at Bethlehem, Pennsylvania, with the Moravians. [Here follows a
glowing account of their schools, etc.] The
best site for a French colony would be at the
head of the Ohio, between the Aleghain and
the Monongahela. Let fifty families, part
nobles, part good citizens, come with their servants and farm-hands, mechanics,—in all from
one thousand to twelve hundred persons; with
money enough to buy lands for themselves and
for those who, approved by a two-thirds vote,
may join them, the latter paying, of course,
a proportion of the expenses already incurred.
Fifteen hundred acres will suffice for a farm
that will maintain in comfort each family.
There will be no difficulty in buying land; the

Americans are lazy and bored, often moving from place to place for the sake of change; in the thirty years that the Pennsylvania neighborhood suggested has been settled, it has changed owners two or three times. The sight of money will tempt any American to sell, and off he goes to new country, leaving the newcomer all his improvements.

" The Ohio, Monongahela, and Allegheny rivers are full of fine fish, the forests of game— wild turkies, deer, pigeons, pheasants, etc. Vegetables grow to a size unknown in Europe; in four or five months, the splendid forests will be converted into smiling farms, each producing food enough for thirty persons, besides that for the cattle in the winter. These families, unlike the Americans, will spend the winter in earnest studies and innocent amusements. In the centre of the village build a great temple, with houses for the clergy on either side; at opposite points a palace of justice, and a meeting place; beyond a college and a school for girls. In the middle of this square, put a fountain at the foot of a column instructing posterity as to the motives of the emigrants settled here. Erect a hospital cared for by Sisters of St. Vincent de Paul; workshops where local material can be manufactured for the use of the people, the fifty families of the settlement, governed by twelve administrators, one-fourth reëlected annually; the newcomers, all French, will produce hats and linen and cloth and other useful articles, and as each year will bring new hands, new industries will be introduced. Their products will find ready markets in Kentucky and in the South and the Antilles. The profits can be used to buy land as an endowment for schools, churches, etc. New colonies will rise in other quarters, where new industries will follow—glassmaking, potteries, watchmaking, papermaking, iron works, all supplied with experts from France. All these colonies will unite in building a central city, to be called St. Peter's, where illustrious Frenchmen will be immortalized, by streets, fountains, squares, etc., named Fénelon, Buffon, Paschal, Catinat, Rousseau, Racine, Corneille, La Fontaine, Massillon, Vincent de Paul, Sully, Necker, Montesquieu, Tollendal, Mounier, Clermont-

Tonnerre. Have a bishop and twelve clergymen, five magistrates, twelve heads of business,
a college with professors of medicine, mathematics, botany, chemistry, teachers of music
and drawing; the town reserved for the
proprietors, tradesmen and mechanics will live
in the suburbs; many of the clergymen will
also be teachers; the bishop will be elected by
heads of families, and he will be the head of
a future university, so that the State of Pennsylvania and the United States will benefit
by the example and instruction of this French
colony." The author suggests some improvements in the American government; " let it
divide the country into eight monarchies, or
into a number of small republics, or into a
Southern Monarchy and a Northern Republic,
thus securing justice and moderation which
would be lost in a single great Republic."

In a letter dated Philadelphia, December 15,
1791, he describes his plantation on the Monongahela, and near it the home of another
Frenchman, Montpelier, whose owners have
had a romantic history that fills many pages.
On the advice of Francklin [*sic*] the hero of

the story and his sweetheart sailed for America, were married at the Catholic Church in Philadelphia, went to Fort Pitt, made near it their future home; then after five years (with a fortune inherited in France) built a new house filled with every luxury; not far off was the home of another French family, that of M. de Lassus, with every attraction, thus offering to Americans the best examples of good taste, and to other French exiles the advantage of other countrymen near by. One such, M. Audrain, has for five or six years lived at Fort Pitt, and helped his countrymen ruined by the Scioto Company's failure.

The letters of Lezay Marnezia are interesting as a typical example of the dreams of exiled Frenchmen, for a home in America, as a refuge from the storms in France. Impracticable as his schemes seem to-day, still they no doubt attracted the notice of some of those Frenchmen who did come to the United States and made a valuable addition to its population.

Lezay Marnezia [Claude François Adrien, Marquis de], born in Metz, France, August

24, 1735, died in Besançon, November 9, 1800, was captain in the King's Regiment, retired to his estate, abolished " corvées et mainmorte " there, advocated in the assembly equal taxation and suppression of feudal privileges; joined the left, and left France in 1790, taking workingmen, farmers, and artists, to found a colony in Pennsylvania; spent a year in try-ing to do so, and after its failure returned by way of England to France; then went to Switzerland and to France finally. Among many writings, he published a letter to M. Adriani, merchant, Pittsburg, describing his stay in Pennsylvania [Paris, 1797]; he pub-lished in Paris, 1792, his " Voyage." His son wrote a book, " Considérations sur les Etats de Massachusetts et Pennsylvanie," Paris, 1795. Another son who had accompanied the father to Pennsylvania, became a French Senator in 1852 and died in that year.

XI

FRENCH PLAN OF EDUCATION IN THE UNITED STATES

DUPONT DE NEMOURS helped, under Vergennes, in the recognition of the United States by France, became secretary of the assembly of notables, and a member of the Etats généraux, as representative from Nemours, in 1795, one of the Conseil des Anciens, an exile to the United States in 1797, remaining there until 1802; he left France again in 1815, joining his sons, who had established themselves in business in Delaware, and died there in 1817. He published in Paris in 1812 a work on National Education in the United States.[1] It was, he says, in his Preface, written in 1800 at the request of Mr. Jefferson, then Vice-President of the United States. He says: " The United States are more advanced in educa-

---

[1] Dupont de Nemours: "Sur l'Éducation Nationale dans les États Unis d'Amérique," 2e edition, Paris, 1812.

tion than most other countries. There are many schools for children, almost every one learns to read, write and reckon. Only four per thousand do not, while in Spain, Portugal, and Italy, hardly one-sixth can do so; in Germany and France more than one-third, in Poland, only two per cent., and in Russia not 1 per cent. England, Holland, and the Protestant cantons of Switzerland come next to the United States. He urges Congress to offer prizes for the best books for education. Their sale will bring in an income of $50,000, while $10,000 will pay for the books and the prizes.

He advises the establishment of colleges in every county, or in less populous neighborhoods for every group of two or more. Free scholarships should be given according to the votes of the students, to be held for seven years. Six professors can teach in each college, seven classes, ten courses, twenty sciences, and forty methods of studying them will provide a programme. Each class will vote for the prizes to be awarded to its members, and at the end of seven years the winners will be made free students at the University. He gives tables of the distribution of hours and studies, and a schedule of salaries:

One president at $500 a year; six professors at $300, $1,800; two supervisors, at $200, $400; one cook at $200; three servants at $150, $450; prizes, repairs, etc., $150; total $3,500; for ten colleges, $35,000.

One hundred and forty free scholarships, fourteen for each college, at $150, $56,000; special schools, $10,500; fifty free students in schools, $10,000; cost of a college in Virginia, $76,500.

Students' annual fees, $150; students other than free scholars, $125; students for open courses, $100.

The special schools will be those of Theology, Law, Medicine, Arts, which with the colleges and the primary and secondary schools will constitute the University of North America.

The course in the Medical School should cover five years, the Law School three years, the School of Social Science three years, the School of Mathematics three years. Each

State and the United States should each have a Council of Instruction, to be in close touch with the Legislatures and Executive.

This paper is dated New York, 15 June, 1800.

XII

FRENCH COLONIES IN THE UNITED STATES: GALLIPOLIS, OHIO; ASYLUM, PENNSYLVANIA

THE story of the French colony at Gallipolis is told by McMaster in the second volume, pp. 146, etc., of his History of the United States. "It is no wonder that the sad experience of the French emigrants attracted to that place by the Scioto Land Company and its agent in France, Barlow, and its manager in New York, Duer, long deterred any similar attempts. Barlow went to Paris just after the opening of the French Revolution, and began to sell title deeds to estates in the West at five shillings the acre. Tempted by his exaggerated descriptions of the land, the soil, and the climate, no taxes, no military service, no soldiers to live on the people, no wolves, or foxes, no bears or tigers, the land on the shores of the Ohio, called the Beautiful, in its waters enormous fish, on its banks majestic trees, out of whose sides ran sugar, and bushes with berries yielding wax,—with such a picture before them, numbers of Frenchmen made haste to sell what little stores of worldly goods they had and buy lands in America. Before the close of 1791 five hundred emigrants from Havre, Bordeaux, Nantes, and Rochelle, were on the sea. Some could build coaches, some make perukes, some carve, others gild. The first shipload started with words of encouragement from Barlow, under the charge of a man named Boulogne, who was bidden to inform the gentlemen proprietors of lands on the Scioto, that each was to receive a house lot and a right to the commons in the city they were about to found. They were to be the fathers and founders of a nation. In May, 1790, after a voyage of seventy-two days, the first shipload brought to Alexandria, Virginia, two hundred of the newcomers, and one hundred and twenty arrived a little later. After the hardships of their long voyages, came the discovery that the agent in charge was a knave. Some had lost clothing, some baggage, which they asked in vain that the Scioto Company

should reimburse them. A few took refuge
with the French Minister and were sent home.
The rest, after endless hardships, reached the
promised land, only to find that the sellers had
no title to the land. At the end of a year
food gave out and they were forced to beg or
buy it from the emigrants that went by on the
river. In the spring of 1792 the Indians
carried off one of their number. Filled with
alarm, some went to Detroit, some to Kaskaskia,
and of the few that remained, travellers gave
a sad description. In 1795 Congress gave
them twenty-four thousand acres of land opposite the mouth of the Little Sandy River, and
three years later twelve hundred more, known
as the French Grant." The site of the Scioto
Company was within the territory which
Franklin nearly forty years before had pointed
out for colonization.

As early as 1754, soon after the Albany
Convention of that year, Franklin wrote a
paper " For Settling two Western Colonies in
North America " (printed in Smyth's Franklin, vol. iii, p. 358, etc.), in which he argued
that this would prevent " the dreaded junction

of the French settlements in Canada with those in Louisiana," and suggested that " two charters be granted, each for some considerable part of the lands west of Pennsylvania and the Virginian mountains, to a number of the nobility and gentry of Britain, with such Americans as shall join them in contributing to the settlement of these lands, either by paying a proportion of the expense of making such settlements, or by actually going thither in person and settling themselves and families. That by such charters it be granted that every actual settler be entitled to a tract of —— acres for himself, and —— acres for every poll in the family he carries with him; and that every contribution of —— guineas be entitled to a quantity of land equal to the share of a single settler," etc. A small fort on the Buffalo Creek on the Ohio, and another at the mouth of the Tioga, on the south side of Lake Erie, where a post should be formed, and a town erected, for the trade of the lakes, would suffice. The river Scioto, which runs into the Ohio, is supposed the fittest seat for the other colony, there being for forty miles on each side of it a body of all rich land, the finest spot in its bigness in all North America, and has the particular advantage of sea coal in plenty (even above ground in two places), for fuel, when the woods shall be destroyed. Again, in 1772 (Smyth's Franklin, vol. v, p. 479, etc.) Franklin urged the confirmation of Walpole's grant for a settlement on the Ohio River. He said that the lands in question are excellent, the climate temperate; native grapes, silk-worms, and mulberry-trees are everywhere; hemp grows spontaneously in the valleys and low lands; iron ore is plenty in the hills, and no soil is better adapted for the culture of tobacco, flax, and cotton.

In " Travels in America," by Thomas Twining [reprinted, New York, 1894], the young Englishman speaks of meeting at Mr. Bingham's in Philadelphia, in 1795, Count de Noailles and Count Tilley, and the celebrated Mons. Volney, of whom he says: " He told me he should probably publish some account of America. He examined things very minutely. I cannot say I was much pleased with Mons. Volney. He was cold and satirical. I concluded that the political troubles in which he had been engaged, and the persecution which had banished him from his country, had caused this splenetic unsociableness or increased a constitutional irritability. He was little pleased with America, and where he was not pleased he expressed himself with much severity. As a philosopher he might be expected to see with less surprise and dissatisfaction the imperfections of a new State, so remote from the improvements and influence of Europe; and as the guest of America he might be expected to repay her hospitality with more urbanity and indulgence. It appeared to me that Monsieur Volney was disappointed because he had unreasonably expected too much, and unjust in blaming a society that could hardly be other than it was." Twining also mentions seeing " a tall gentleman in a blue coat, pointed out as M. Talleyrand," walking on Chestnut Street, in Philadelphia.

VOLNEY'S TRAVELS IN THE UNITED STATES

Volney says that the land of the Scioto Company offered in Paris at six livres an acre was really worth six or seven sous an acre, but partly misled by Brissot's book, partly by the growing disorders in France, in 1791 quite a number of purchasers sailed from Havre, Bordeaux, Nantes, and Rochelle, for their new home. In 1795 Volney could get no particulars of the colony at Gallipolis, and made the journey thither to see it. He heard the story from the settlers and saw the poor results of their efforts to make a living—only fifty were left. He visited Vincennes on the Wabash, where a colony of French " Canadians " had settled before the American Revolution. " After being by turns French and Spanish and American subjects, the government, in 1792, in compensation for their losses, gave them four hundred acres for each taxpayer, and one hundred more for every man who could bear arms; but hunters rather than farmers, they sold their lands to Americans for one-tenth of their value and took payment in goods at far more than their real value. Reduced to poverty, the old settlers complain, but in vain, of laws they do not understand, and judges who do not understand them. The Americans charge them with indolence and ignorance; there were no schools until the French Revolution sent them a missionary,—yet of ninety French settlers, hardly six could read or write, while of every hundred Americans, ninety can do so. Largely sprung from French soldiers sent to Canada, they still long for a military government. The same conditions exist with the French settlers in Illinois, Kaskaskia, Cahokias, Prairie du Rocher, St. Louis; within five or six years the Americans have become owners of all the good land. Only a hundred and fifty French families were reported by Sargent, secretary of the Northwest Territory, in 1790. The same conditions existed at Fort Detroit, most of the French going across the boundary into King George's Canada, just as those further southwest to New Orleans and other parts of Louisiana." Volney regrets that the French colony of Gallipolis had not gone to one of the old French settlements and strengthened it.

Volney saw Gallipolis in 1796, and in his " View of the Climate and Soil of the United States " says he was struck with the wild appearance and the sallow complexions, thin visages and sickly looks and uneasy air of its inhabitants. One of the settlers at Gallipolis was Jean Jules Le Moyne de Villers, a native of Paris. He settled in Washington, Pennsylvania, about 1797, became a leading physician, and was a generous benefactor of local education. His descendants are active and useful citizens.

There was a settlement made by the French under the old claim on the site of the present city of Erie, Pennsylvania, where they built a rude log fort called " Presq'Isle," the first one of the chain of forts built by the French from the St. Lawrence to the Ohio. Not a trace was left forty years after its capture by the British, in the old French War.

The Centennial of Gallipolis, celebrated October 16–19, 1890, by the Ohio State Archeological and Historical Society, is fully described in its volume (Columbus, Ohio, 1895), with illustrations — the city of 1890, views of the cabins built 1791, its public square in 1790 and in 1846, a map of 1791, and maps of the purchases of the Ohio

and Scioto Companies and that issued by the
latter in Paris to be shown to intending settlers.
An exposition of relics brought together quite
a goodly array of articles of furniture, etc.,
brought out by the original settlers and still
cherished by their descendants and their
owners.

Mr. John L. Vance read a paper on " The
French Settlement and Settlers of Gallipolis "
(pp. 45–81); he quotes at length a letter of
M. Meutelle, one of the original settlers,
printed in the *American Pioneer*, Cincinnati,
April, 1843, and an earlier letter from Mr.
Le Turc, a Gallipolis merchant, dated July 6,
1792, with a gloomy view of the prospect. It
was largely through Duponceau's help that
Congress made " the French Grant " of
twenty-four thousand acres opposite the Little
Sandy, for the people of Gallipolis. He gives
a sketch " map of the four-acre lots drawn by
the inhabitants of Gallipolis January 20,
1791," with a numeral list of the town lots,
with their original disposition, making in all
two hundred and thirty-four, and all names are
French. There is also a paper of December

14, 1795, giving the plan of distribution of the town- and out-lots. Reference is made to the account given by John Heckewelder of his visit in 1792, in company with General Putnam, when they found skilled workmen, goldsmiths and watchmakers, stonecutters and sculptors, whose productions were sold as far as New Orleans, a glassworker making thermometers and barometers, and chemists making nitric acid, phosphorus, etc. There is also a long extract from H. M. Brackenridge's Recollections. He stopped at Gallipolis previous to 1795, with Dr. Saugrain, chemist, natural philosopher, and physician, a royalist like most of the settlers, making a bold struggle against great difficulties. A school started twenty years later, was called Gallia Academy, and Gallia County perpetuates the nationality of the French settlers of Gallipolis. In 1824 Lafayette visited it, as Louis Philippe and his brothers did at a much earlier date, on their way to New Orleans. To-day it is a prosperous town, but with few descendants of the original French settlers. A translation is given of Manasseh Cutler's "Description," etc., for Barlow's use in floating the Scioto Company in France, published in Paris in 1789, from the original English version issued in Salem, Massachusetts, in 1787. The copy used bears on its title-page the name of one of the French settlers, dated 1805. An account is given (p. 123) of the Society of the Scioto, organized in Paris by Barlow, in 1789, to which he sold three million acres, at $1.14 per acre. A land office was opened in Paris, and maps with glowing descriptions of the lands on the Ohio and the Scioto were issued. Gallipolis was laid out, and one of the original deeds is still preserved there. Full details are given of the transfer to the Ohio Company, and of the complicated difficulties that led to the failure of these great land schemes, of Duponceau's efforts to secure from Congress relief for his defrauded countrymen, and abstracts of the laws passed for the purpose.

Volney, after an imprisonment of ten months in France, sailed in 1795 for the United States, remaining there until 1798, when the " epidemic animosity against the

French " compelled him to leave the country. In the English edition of his " View, etc., of the United States," (London, 1804, pp. 355, etc.), he gives an account of Gallipolis, or the French colony on the Ohio. He attributes much of the success of the Scioto Company's scheme in Paris to Brissot's account in his Travels in the United States. The emigration began in 1791, through Havre, Bordeaux, Nantes, and Rochelle.

Volney on his arrival in Philadelphia, in 1795, inquired in vain after the colony, so in the following summer he travelled from Philadelphia through Virginia, in an open boat down the Great Kanhaway [*sic*] into the Ohio, and at last reached the village of Gallipolis. There he found two rows of little white houses, built on the flat summit of the bank of the Ohio. He found the place wild and unkempt, the people thin, sickly, and uneasy. The houses were nothing but huts made of trunks of trees, plastered with clay and covered with shingles, whitewashed, but damp and badly sheltered from the weather. About five hundred settlers, all of them mechanics, artists, or tradesmen in easy circumstances, had come in 1791 and 1792, to New York, Philadelphia, and Baltimore. Each had paid twenty or twenty-four guineas for passage, and their journey by land in France and America had cost as much more. After an Indian assault, the greater number abandoned the place, some removing to Louisiana. Then after more litigation, the remaining settlers obtained a tract of nine hundred and twelve acres from the Ohio Company. In 1795 Congress granted twenty thousand acres to the poor pillaged Frenchmen, and Volney found them trying to secure a livelihood on their new home. Later he visited the French colonies on the Mississippi and Lake Erie. At St. Vincent the French settlers had been established for sixty years, and there as with those at Kaskaskia, Cahokia, Rocky Meadows, and St. Louis, discouragement, apathy, and wretchedness prevailed.

André Michaux's "Travels into Kentucky, 1793–96," and François André Michaux's "Travels to the West of the Allegheny Mountains in the States of Ohio, Kentucky, and Tennessee," 1802, have been reprinted by

Thwaites in vol. iii of his "Early Western Travels," Cleveland, Ohio, 1904.

The son presented to the American Philosophical Society the father's field notes, and these were printed by the American Philosophical Society in 1889. Although Michaux's comment on the French settled in the West is unfavorable, yet he records the number of Frenchmen who became prominent and useful citizens of the West—Lucas at Pittsburg, Lacassagne at Louisville, Tardiveau, Hourie, and Depauw at Danville. Father and son both visited Gallipolis; the former speaks of it as "that unfortunate colony; of the six hundred persons who came there to settle, only one hundred and fifty remained in 1793." In 1802 the son visited Gallipolis and found that only thirty families had gone to the lands granted by Congress, while most of the original log houses were in ruins, the former owners having gone elsewhere, some to New Orleans, others to Pittsburg and points in Western Pennsylvania. Thwaites says that in 1893 Gallipolis had grown into a flourishing town, through the energy of the American and

German settlers, and but three families descendants of the French colonists lived there.

THE FRENCH COLONY OF ASYLUM IN PENNSYLVANIA

Rochefoucauld, in vol. i, p. 151, of his Travels in the United States, gives an account of his visit to the colony of " Azyl " in Pennsylvania. It is perhaps the earliest description of an attempt to colonize French royalist exiles, made under auspices that at the outset promised success. Rochefoucauld gives the names of the principal settlers—De Blacons, a deputy in the Constituent Assembly from Dauphine, and his wife, Mdlle. de Maulde; they were keeping a store, in partnership with M. Colin, formerly the Abbé de Sevigné; M. de Montulé, captain of cavalry; his cousin, Mme. de Sybert, of St. Domingo; De Bec de Lièvre, in partnership with the Messieurs de la Roue, officers of the French army; M. Beaulieu, captain of infantry in France, served in the Pulaski Legion in the American War of Independence, keeping a tavern; M. Bayard, planter from St. Domingo, now with wife and children and some negroes who came with them; M. de Noailles, of St. Domingo; M. d'Audelot, of Franche-Comté, formerly an officer in the French army, then a farmer; Dupetit Thouars, officer of the French navy, now farming; his companion in his adventurous escape from Brazil, M. Norès; Mr. Keating (the founder of a well-known family in Philadelphia), M. Renaud, an exile from St. Domingo; M. Carlier, Canon of Quercy; M. Prevost, of Paris, well known for his active charitable work there, now a farmer on his little property on the North Branch of the Susquehanna; Mme. d'Autrepont, with her sons, working for daily bread, like all the members of the colony.

One fault of the French settlers was their unwillingness to learn the language or conform to the customs of their neighbors, the old American settlers. The other, said Rochefoucauld, is the need of more and better working-people, to make the somewhat unfavorable site at least as prosperous as the other farm settlements. The Duke's hopes for the French colony at Asylum were not realized, and its failure is described by later travellers and in the account given by a resident of to-day.

Rochefoucauld mentions all the Frenchmen he met on his long journey, mostly individual settlers, trying, as in South Carolina, to introduce home industries, but few of them succeeded or left any lasting trace of their residence. Mrs. Murray in her account of Asylum says that the thirty houses built for the settlers had chimneys, doors, staircases, window-glass, shutters, and piazzas and summer-houses, all unknown luxuries to the few neighboring old residents. Some quaint little shops were on the public square with a small chapel and a theatre, as well as a bakery, all evidence of French needs.

Asylum, near Wilkes-Barre, Pennsylvania, was planned by the Vicomte Louis de Noailles, a brother-in-law of Lafayette, and the Marquis Omer Talon; it was a land company owning a large tract on the North Branch of the Susquehanna. Established in 1794, on land sold to the Company by Morris and Nicholson, it secured a tract of two thousand acres, and a M. Boulogne was the active manager until he was drowned in 1796 in Sullivan County and buried at Asylum. The first settlers came in 1793, among them Dupetit Thouars, later killed in command of a man-of-war at the battle of the Nile. Noailles was employed by Robert Morris, but soon left to take part in the French attack on Havana, and died of the wounds received in action. A Catholic church was built, and a large house put up, it was said for the King and Queen of France, when they should make their escape from captivity and seek safety in shelter among their loyal friends at Asylum.

Rochefoucauld in his Travels describes it as he saw it on his visit in 1795. A year later an English traveller, Weld, visited it and tells what he saw in his Travels. Wilson, the ornithologist, was there in 1804 and refers to it in his poem describing his pedestrian tour to Niagara. Louis Philippe and his brother came there too from Philadelphia. John Keating, an exile from St. Domingo, was one of the settlers for a time and remained the agent of the Company in Philadelphia and wound up its business. He was the first of a family well known in Philadelphia and still affiliated with France. Some of the colonists returned to France and became men of note; others went to New Orleans, and in ten years the colony was at an end. The Honorable John Laporte, M.C., was the son of one of the colonists. Mr. J. W. Ingham described it in the *New England Magazine*, N. S., vol. xxxi, pp. 81, etc., 1904–05. "Exiled from France and from St. Domingo, thousands of Frenchmen sought shelter in the United States."

"The Story of Some French Refugees and their Colony of Azilum," 1793–1800, by Louise Welles Montgomery, Athens, Pennsylvania, 1903, is the local version of their trials. The original plot of their settlement is in the Bradford County Historical Society. Omer Talon came to Philadelphia in 1792, and took the oath of allegiance to the State of Pennsylvania. He joined in Philadelphia the Vicomte de Noailles, who was in business with William Bingham, and had bought land from Robert Morris. Their agent selected eight lots of three hundred acres each in Luzerne County on the North Branch of the Susquehanna, for a French colony. They also bought one hundred thousand acres of wild land, on the Loyalsock; in 1794 they organized a land company on the basis of a capital stock of a million acres, in five thousand shares of two hundred acres each. In 1801 the Company was reorganized, and later on the land was sold by trustees. Talon and Dupetit Thouars and Boulogne were active managers. Some of the roads built by Omer Talon are still in use, and one is to-day known as " The Old French Road." A weekly express to Philadelphia was maintained for several years. The Duc de Rochefoucauld describes the place as he saw it in 1795—a settlement in the wilds made for French people of position at home.

The deeds conveying property mentioned some of the advantages of the properties. Mrs. Murray prints an agreement by which Sophia de Sibert sold Nos. 416 and 417 of the Asylum Company's property to Gui de Noailles, and describes the house as having fireplaces, the garden a number of fruit trees, young Lom-

10

bardy poplars and weeping willows, and a lattice summer house, and a nursery of nine hundred apple trees, with a gristmill and a barn that might be altered into a dwelling-house.

Among the relics brought from France there was a beautiful illuminated missal, used in the religious services in the log chapel, later given to a priest in Tonawanda, by whom it was taken to Rome and presented to the Vatican Museum. Even those of the settlers who returned to France gave accounts of the Susquehanna Valley which later attracted settlers whose descendants still live in Bradford County, Pennsylvania, notably the Piollets and the Delpeuchs.

The fate of the originators of "Azylum" was very sad. Noailles died of his wounds in a successful naval engagement off Havana; Dupetit Thouars fell in the Battle of the Nile, and Omer Talon returned to France and died in an insane asylum; De Blacons too returned, became a member of the National Assembly, and died by his own hand; Fromentin, once priest, became a judge in Florida; Beaulieu left descendants now known as Boileau, scattered through Pennsylvania.

In 1801 John Brevost advertised in the Wilkes-Barre *Gazette* that he would open at Asylum a school for teaching the French language, " which within a hundred years has become the common tongue of Europe; is spoken by two large regions of the continent, and which the reward of a sincere friendship between the American and French nations will render necessary to young gentlemen who intend to follow the political or mercantile life; " his price was sixty bushels of wheat a year, but he soon moved to New Orleans.

The list of taxables at Asylum for the year 1796 (the earliest known) has a goodly array of French names, but it is pathetic to follow the decrease in successive years, showing the scattering of the settlers. " The French at Asylum " are the subjects of a paper by the Reverend David Craft, printed by the Wyoming Historical Society, in vol. viii of its Proceedings, in 1902, following an earlier paper by him of 1898, in vol. v, for 1900. It describes actual visits and the results of a careful inspection of the traces of the settlement of 1795.

Of the " great " house, where Omer Talon lived in generous hospitality, entertaining travelling Frenchmen, and caring for his neighbors, not a trace is left, while the gardens and orchards have all disappeared, and all that they were is told in Alexander Wilson's verse:

"Gaul's exiled royalists, a pensive train,
   Here raise the hut and clear the rough domain,"

while of their leaders, there are remembered only Noailles and Dupetit Thouars, and that for their heroic death in the service of their country.

In Alexander Graydon's Memoirs (Harrisburg, 1811) he says: " A letter about the year 1790 or 1791 introduced to me Mr. Talon, then engaged with the Viscomte de Noailles in establishing a settlement on the North Branch of the Susquehanna, and to which they gave the name of Assylum [sic]. He several times passed through Harrisburg. Mr. Talon fully justified to my conception the favorable idea of a Frenchman of rank. I have seldom seen a gentleman with whose manners I was more pleased. Though he spoke but little English, and I less French, yet from the knowledge we had of each other's language, we contrived to make ourselves mutually understood. On one of his visits to Harrisburg he was attended by not less than ten or a dozen gentlemen, all adventurers in the new establishment, from which they had just returned on their way to Philadelphia. Of these I only recollect the names of M. de Blacons, Captain Keating, and Captain Boileau. Captain Keating was an Irishman, and Captain Boileau had been among the troops which had served in this country. M. Blacons expatiated on a projected road from Assylum to Philadelphia, which required nothing but the consent of the Legislature, to be completed out of hand. Talon had been adverse to the Revolution in France in all its stages and modifications. He was the person on account of whose courteous reception General Washington had been roundly taken to task by the Citizen Genet. The Duke de la Rochefoucauld gives some particulars of the

Assylum settlement, humorously called by some of the settlers, *refugium peccatorum,* and enumerates the families which had established themselves there. The settlement is now entirely abandoned by the French; a tract more rugged and mountainous could hardly be found. It agrees with Mr. Talon's account of it: ' A narrow strip of flat land along the river.' Talon was Avocat General under the old régime, of the family of the one spoken of by Cardinal de Retz."

XIII

FRENCH SETTLEMENT IN IOWA

THERE has been little written about the French settlements in Iowa, chiefly because the French pioneers made few settlements in Iowa that continued and because the immigration since has been slight. Of French communities existing to-day there are but four in the State. Near Waterloo, south and east, there is a community that was known as " Frenchtown " in common parlance, but in the Postal Guide it goes under the name of Gilbertville. There is a French community near Woodstock, a rural agricultural folk. Not far from Sioux City is a little town of Salix, made up almost wholly of French, many of them descendants of Canadian voyageurs who returned from fruitless expeditions up the Missouri River in the fur-trading days and became the pioneers of Woodbury County and the first settlers of Sioux City. In the northern part of Washington County,

Iowa, in the southeastern portion of the State, there is another French community. It is somewhat interfused with other peoples at present. Another French community is the religious brotherhood at the monastery of Melleray, not far from Dubuque, in northeastern Iowa. Of the early settlements, Dubuque contained the greatest number and they constitute to-day a noticeable element in that city. Girard (now McGregor) opposite Prairie du Chien in Wisconsin, Bellevue in Jackson County, and Montrose in Lee County, and St. Mary's, Pottawattamie County, are defunct French settlements. Davenport and Keokuk contain some descendants and originals of the pioneer French stock that first invaded Iowa. Not a few of the Icarians or their descendants are found in Keokuk to-day. The architect of Iowa's capitol was an Icarian, S. Picquenard.[1]

The Socialist colony of Icaria in Iowa is described by Nordhoff in his " Communistic Societies of the United States," New York, 1875, pp. 334, etc., and in an article in the

[1] Letter from Prof. F. I. Herriott, Drake University, Dubuque, Iowa.

London Quarterly Review of June, 1848, pp. 16, etc., and by Hillquist in his " History of Socialism in the United States." He says the founder, Cabet, was born in Dijon in 1788, was a member of the French Assembly in 1834. He bought a million acres in Texas, arrived in New Orleans in 1848, with four hundred followers, and by 1849 had five hundred. The Texas scheme failed, and he next moved to Nauvoo, Illinois, lately abandoned by the Mormons; in 1856 Cabet was expelled, and he died soon after in St. Louis, near which some hundred of his adherents settled, but that colony broke up in 1859. The others had gone to Iowa and established a colony which broke up in 1887, part of it going to California, while the old Icaria ended in 1895. The California colony lasted only a few years, but was followed by many French settlers, to whom is largely due the successful culture of vineyards, olive and fig and peach and other small fruits, which contribute greatly to the prosperity of the State.

" Soon after the last remnant of Mormon population disappeared from Nauvoo there appeared on that historic spot the advance agents of a new colony seeking opportunity to exploit other peculiar theories of social life in this far western country.[1] Nauvoo was an ideal site for such an experiment, and the agents hastily returned to New Orleans with a favorable report and an option on the land for the waiting colonists. These were the Icarians, a considerable body of communists, organized in France by Etienne Cabet of Dijon. The foundation of his dream of absolute equality, as typified in a democratic republic to be called Icaria, was laid in 1830, and by 1847 four hundred thousand names were reported as signed to the Social Compact. A year later, having obtained a large tract of land in Texas, an advance guard of sixty-nine sailed from France to take formal possession; others followed, but from various causes, more particularly the nature of the country and the prevalence of malarial fever, this first colonization was an utter failure, so that when, in 1849, Cabet reached New Orleans and took

[1] Settlement of the Icarians at Nauvoo, p. 347, Parrish's Historic Illinois.

personal command of the entire force, then numbering five hundred, including many women and children, agents were despatched up the Mississippi seeking a more suitable location for permanent settlement.

" In March, 1849, the remnant of the colony, still firm in belief of their dream, began their journey up the river. It proved a fearful one. Cholera broke out and many died. Twenty miles below Nauvoo, ice blocked further passage northward by steamer, and they were compelled to tramp the remainder of the way knee deep in snow and slush, carrying children and sick as best they could. At Nauvoo they found some comfort in the houses still standing as the banished Mormons had left them, yet much suffering remained. The climate was severe, water unwholesome, food costly, indeed nearly impossible to obtain at any price. For months they subsisted entirely upon beans. But in the midst of all this hardship, the spirit of the Icarians remained unbroken. Slowly they built their little commonwealth, a mere child's toy compared to the stately city of their enthusiastic leader's plans, yet ruled by the same laws, controlled by the same ideals, which had made them exiles. Six directors, elected annually, controlled the administration; the laws were made by a general assembly, including all men over twenty. Cabet was elected president year after year, yet exercised little authority, as the title was merely one of honor. The colony was purely communistic, the members putting their possessions, even books and heirlooms, into the common fund. Furniture, tools, and cooking utensils were equally divided; tasks and hours of labor were evenly proportioned. Homes were separate, each family occupying its own house, but the colony school reared the children in common; all ate at one table; individualism was treated as unworthy.

" For a while the community flourished and increased; it became fairly prosperous. By 1855 they had with great industry and self-denial erected mills and workshops, their farms were well tilled, their school ranked among the best in the State. A well-selected library of over six thousand volumes had been established, and a well-organized trained orchestra was the marvel of the neighbors. A weekly magazine was published in three languages, with a wide circulation in the United States and Europe. New members were constantly arriving, among them men and women of culture, accomplished musicians, painters of reputation, a famous civil engineer, a physician of standing in Vienna, an authority on bee culture, Picquenard, afterwards architect of the capitols in Iowa and Illinois; Vallet, a sociologist, Gauvain, officer, teacher, nobleman. Cabet himself was the cause of failure. Late in 1855, tired of being president only in name, he tried to have the constitution revised so as to give him almost dictatorial powers; but this led to a bitter contest. Cabet was deposed at the election, but was restored on his appeal to the voters.

" Later he commanded his old officials not to vacate their positions to those newly elected. This led to a strike by Cabet's loyal followers, who refused to work when the new directors were put in by force by the majority. After a bitter struggle the majority burned Cabet's ' Icaria,' until then their creed, a legal division of the community property was decided upon, and Cabet by vote expelled. One hundred and eighty disciples accompanied him into exile, while eight hundred remained. A week later he died suddenly of apoplexy in St. Louis. His followers located six miles below that city, prospered for a while, then broke up. The majority drifted away from Nauvoo to a tract of land in Iowa. There by 1875 they reached the height of their prosperity, after much struggle, and then a second division separated the younger from the older members, the former drifting to California, the latter clinging to Icaria, until by 1895 the last vestige of their community had perished, almost without a ripple, from mere exhaustion. The California colony lasted a little longer, but that too finally ended from want of the old enthusiasm and of new recruits."

XIV

BONAPARTIST EXILES

AMONG French exiles to America who became prominent on their return to France, were Marshal Grouchy, Lefebvre Desnouettes, Clausel, later governor general of Algiers and marshal, Lackanal, later minister of education under Napoleon. In 1817 Parmentier obtained a grant of land in Alabama for French refugees, who left Philadelphia and settled at St. Stephen's, on the Tombigbee; at the suggestion of Comte Real it was called Demopolis. German Redemptioners were hired to work the land, but it was finally abandoned after vain efforts to introduce the culture of vines, olives, etc., leaving debts and quarrels with neighbors. Of the settlers Clouis, once secretary of the Duc de Rovigo, died in Mobile in 1845, and Chaudron in 1846. Chaudron had lived in Philadelphia, delivered an oration on Washington before the Masonic Order, and was a frequent contributor to French journals.

"The Napoleonic Exiles in America; a Study in American Diplomatic History, 1815–1819," by Jesse S. Reeves, Ph.D. Baltimore. Johns Hopkins Press, September-October, 1905, is No. 9-10 of Series 23 of Johns Hopkins University Studies in History and Political Science. It opens with an account of the unfortunate colonial enterprise called Champs d'Asile, on the banks of the Trinity River, in Texas. Balzac in the third part of " Les Cèlibataires " sketched the purposes and results of the plan of founding a French colony of Napoleon's old soldiers, particularly the remnant of the Old Guard, partly to get them out of Paris and France, to the relief of the newly restored Bourbons, partly to carry out Napoleon's vague plan of seeking an asylum in America. Joseph Bonaparte did so for sixteen years, living in or near Philadelphia from 1816 until 1832. Of the other soldiers of Napoleon sent into exile, the first to land was Marshal Grouchy, who reached Baltimore in January, 1816,—published in Philadelphia, in 1818, his account of Waterloo, and in 1820 a pamphlet on Napoleon's Memoirs. Later came the Lallemands, Lefebvre Desnouettes, Rigaud, Clausel, Real, Galabert, Schultz, Combes, Jordan, Latapie, Vorster, Douarche, Charrasin, Taillade, Défourni, and others of less rank. Lakanal brought a letter from Lafayette to Jefferson, and first settled in Gallatin County, near Vevay, Indiana.

A company was formed in Philadelphia in 1816 to secure a grant of land for settlement and cultivation of vine and olive. The secretary, Colonel Parmentier, secured the grant for " The French Agricultural and Manufacturing Society," and the Tombigbee Association. General Charles Lallemand was elected president, and most of the shareholders were the French officers of Napoleon's army, whose names are given above. The site selected was on the Tombigbee River in Alabama. One hundred and fifty sailed from Philadelphia in 1817, and later a still larger number; all were heartily welcomed. " Demopolis " was surveyed, but being outside the grant, " Aigleville " took its place. " Marengo," as the name of the county, still preserves this Napoleonic idea.

The leading colonist was Lefebvre Desnouettes, with a farm of five hundred acres, and a log cabin, which he called his sanctuary; in it (tradition says) was a large bronze statue of Napoleon, at its base the swords and pistols Lefebvre had taken in battle, and on the walls the colors of the Emperor. Peniers and Raoul and Clouis were his neighbors. The colony soon melted away, and Lallemand planned another in Texas. Meantime Hyde de Neuville, then French Minister in Washington, was frightened by the plan of a Napoleonic invasion of Mexico, where Joseph Bonaparte was to be made Emperor. It really had little to do with the plans for the Texas colony, which landed in Galveston in 1818, welcomed by Lafitte, and all, some three or four hundred, soon left for the site of the new colony on Trinity River, where fort and blockhouses were built, ground was cleared, and a proclamation of its plan issued. It was published in Paris, and one hundred thousand francs were subscribed there for the colony. Beranger wrote a hymn in its honor, but the colony melted away at the threat of a Spanish invading force. It retreated to Galveston, joined D'Auvray, a Frenchman who planned wresting Texas from Spain, but a storm wrecked the place, and Lafitte rescued them. The younger Lallemand returned to Philadelphia and after marrying a niece of Girard, went with the elder brother to Europe; Lakanal, after a hard experience in the West, went to France and became a person of much importance.

M. Georges Bertin gives a very clear account of a leading French exile in his " Joseph Bonaparte in America," 1815–1832 (Paris, 1893). He describes his estate at Bordentown, and his large purchase of wild land in New York from Le Ray de Chaumont, made in 1814 in France, when sales of smaller tracts were made to Real, Caulaincourt, and later in 1816 to Grouchy, Desfourneaux, and others. Joseph Bonaparte had, before the fall of the Empire, loaned two hundred thousand francs to Le Ray, and in payment took the lands on the Black River which he saw for the first time in 1818. There he saw a cottonmill, an iron forge, and a papermill, and was delighted with the improvements made in the last four years. He made more purchases of land from Le Ray, making a total investment of $120,000, partly in payment of the original loan of $40,000, and partly in diamonds, carried from his French home at Morfontaine, hidden in Switzerland, and returned there to his agent Maillard. He built a house, gave hunting parties on his estate of one hundred and fifty thousand acres, and fished and sailed on his lake of twelve hundred acres, filled with wooded islands. His daughter Charlotte made sketches, of which some were lithographed. The Legislature of New York passed an act enabling him to hold the land. The Emperor in St. Helena approved of his brother's plans, and said that if he had gone to America, he would have gathered around him all his family, and with the millions he had given them, in a year he would have had sixty thousand Frenchmen with a capital of twenty million dollars, and America would have been a true asylum for those who had fled from the system that had triumphed in

Europe, and from which they would send forth sound doctrines. Joseph made homes for some of the French officers exiled to the United States, but in 1829 he offered to sell land that had cost him five dollars an acre in 1814, for from three to seven dollars an acre, and said there were a thousand settlers with roads, mills, villages, etc. In 1835 he sold his land to Mr. John Lafarge of New York for eighty thousand dollars, a heavy loss on his original investment. He spent one hundred and fifty thousand dollars on his Bordentown estate, and the expenses of living there made deep inroads on his diminishing fortune, while he supplied the money to establish in New York the *Courrier des Etats Unis,* in charge of Lacoste, formerly an officer in the French army, and an aid of Marshal Gérard at Waterloo. Hyde de Neuville on his arrival as French Minister to the United States, in 1816, found here, as he tells us in his Memoirs, many Napoleonic exiles whose movements he reported to his government. In New York were Regnault de St. Jean d'Angely, Quinet, and Real; in Philadelphia, Grouchy, Clausel,

Garnier de Saintes, and near by Joseph Bonaparte with his associates and frequent visitors, among them Colonel Behr, who was planning for him a kingdom in Mexico, helped by Lakanal. Napoleon at St. Helena heard of the report and laughed at the idea. Lakanal was really in earnest at work as president of the University of Louisiana, a post he held until his return to France.

General Bernard, according to Neuville, one of the conspirators, was glad to find employment as an engineer in the service of the United States, and in grateful acknowledgment, named his son, born here in 1819, Columbus. Returned to France after the Revolution of 1830, he died there holding the office of minister of war. Grouchy published in Philadelphia, in 1815, his criticism of Gourgaud's account of Waterloo, and again, in 1820, that of the authenticity of the Memoirs attributed to Napoleon. He was one of the owners of land on the Black River, New York, and thus had business dealings with Joseph Bonaparte. Another of his visitors was General Vandamme, in whose division Joseph Bonaparte had a regi-

ment. He, too, lived in Philadelphia, until
with Arnault and Bory Saint Vincent, he returned to France in 1820. The Lallemands
were warmly welcomed by Joseph Bonaparte,
and Neuville said they were leaders in the
Texas colony and in the plans for a Napoleonic
confederation in Mexico.

Lefebvre Desnouettes was shipwrecked on
his voyage home and lost on the Irish coast.
Charles Lallemand, after the failure of the
colony in Texas, opened a school and thus
maintained himself until his return to France,
where Louis Philippe gave him an important
command. Charles J. Ingersoll has recorded
in his " History of the Second War with Great
Britain," many details of his personal acquaintance with " the Comte de Survilliers," as the
ex-king of Spain chose to call himself. Two
of his friends, Lallemand and Rigau, both old
soldiers under the great Napoleon, had charge
of the four hundred men who went to the
French colony " Champs d'Asile." Rigau
died in New Orleans, leaving a daughter whose
descendants include Mme. Jules Ferry, Colonel
Charras, Scheurer Kestner, and Charles

Floquet. A detailed account of this French colony in Texas, was published in Paris in 1820.

Bertin cites from Ingersoll, the following names of Frenchmen who were visitors at Joseph Bonaparte's: Grouchy, Clausel, Bernard, Charles and Henry Lallemand, Lefebvre Desnouettes, Vandamme, Combes, Girardin, Latapie, the sons of Grouchy, Regnault de St. Jean d'Angely, Real, Miot de Melito, Lakanal, Quinet, two sons of Fouché, a son of Marshal Ney, the son of Marshal Lannes, a very fair showing of the French officers of Napoleon, from time to time in America. Lafayette himself on his triumphal tour of the United States in 1824, was more than once a guest of Joseph Bonaparte. Many of his visitors returned to France and received offices from Louis Philippe, thus reducing his adherents in the vain struggle to restore his nephew, the son of the great Napoleon, to the throne. While he was supporting the French paper in New York he was asked to help others in France and England, and to get money for this purpose, he tried to sell his Black River property to Girard, but the death of the latter turned the sale in another direction. He kept in close touch with the attacks on the government of Louis Philippe and noted that of Cabet, later founder of Icaria, the unsuccessful colony in the West. In 1832 he left the United States, after a stay of seventeen years, and a farewell reception from the President of the United States, an honor not accorded him until he was about to leave the country. Coming to it an exile, he had planned to bring together many of his fellow exiles, but some of them returned to France to take service under Louis Philippe, while others returned to take up again the apparently hopeless effort to put a Bonaparte on the throne of France, and a few remained to lead quiet lives as good American citizens.

" The French Grant in Alabama; a History of the Founding of Demopolis," by Gaius Whitfield, Jr. (From the Transactions of the Alabama Historical Society, Reprint No. 16.) Montgomery, Ala., 1904, refers to accounts in:

1. Pickett's History of Alabama, entitled, " Modern French Colony in Alabama."

2. Professor Thomas Chalmers McCorvey's "The Vine and Olive Colony," in *Alabama Historical Reporter*, Tuscaloosa, April, 1885.

3. Anne Bozeman Lyon's article on "The Bonapartists in Alabama," in the *Southern Home Journal*, Memphis, March, 1900, and reprinted in the *Gulf States Historical Magazine*, Montgomery, March, 1903.

4. Articles in the Demopolis *Express*, by J. W. Beeson.

It cites from *Niles' Register* (note p. 324) an estimate that not less than thirty thousand French emigrants came to the United States, and a correction that it could not be three thousand. An association was organized in Philadelphia to establish a colony in the West, but its agents, Pennier and Meslier, could not find a suitable site. Meantime it sent Colonel Nicholas Parmentier to Washington to petition Congress for a tract of land. They decided, finally, to settle near the confluence of the Black Warrior and Tombigbee Rivers, in what was then the Mississippi Territory. It was near Mobile, where there were many sympathizers, and not far from Louisiana, where they hoped to get help towards their plans to restore Napoleon to his empire. Congress granted them the tract by Act of March 3, 1817, " four contiguous townships, each six miles square in the Mississippi Territory, at two dollars per acre, payable fourteen years after a contract with agents of the late emigrants from France, associated for a settlement in the United States, with provisions for cultivating vines, etc., no patent to be issued until payment had been made, nor to any one person for more than six acres." Parmentier sailed from Philadelphia and reported his arrival in a letter dated Mobile Bay, May 26, 1817, published in the *National Intelligencer* on the following July 17.

It was decided to settle where Demopolis now stands, and the name of Marengo was given to the county. The emigrants came by way of Mobile and by the Ohio, chose lots, erected cabins, and at the suggestion of Count Real, one of the Philadelphia incorporators who never came to Alabama, named it Demopolis. The contract signed with the Secretary of the Treasury conveyed the land for $184,-

320, to be paid on or before January 8, 1833. It provided for clearing ten acres on each tract, for planting five hundred olive trees within seven years, and for annual reports as to vine and olive cultivation, and with it was a list of nearly four hundred persons to whom allot- ments were made, among them the two sons of Marshal Grouchy, General Lallemand, Colonel Douarche, Colonel Comb, Colonel Jordan, Colonel Vorster, Colonel Galabert, Colonel Rigau, Lakanal, Tulane, Clouis, General Clausel, Colonel Charassin, Colonel Raoul, Colonel Taillade, Bujac, Salaignac, Brugière, General Lefebvre Desnouettes, Ducommun, Melizet, and others still known in Philadelphia and Mobile. Their first town site was found not within their grant, so a second was laid out and called Aigleville. The reports of the agent of the treasury were regularly printed for Congress and described their houses, etc.; but the colonists suffered great hardships, in spite of frequent remittances of money and supplies from France. Their vines and olives were total failures from the unsuitable loca- tion. Some of the settlers went with Lallemand to Texas to establish " Champs d'Azile," but that too failed. In 1820 some of the St. Domingo refugees came from Philadelphia to join the Demopolis colony. In 1822 Congress passed an act to convey title to those who might pay for their land. Their agent, Charles Villars, said there were three hundred and twenty-seven persons in the colony, eighty-one actual planters, with eleven hundred acres in full cultivation, and fifteen hundred by lease; ten thousand vines in full growth, and more than $160,000 spent. The Treasury Agent reported, in 1827, seven thousand four hundred and fourteen acres in vine, corn, cotton, small grain, etc., and in 1828 another agent explained the reasons for the failure of the vines, and in another report described the receipt of vines imported from France, losses on the way, after planting, by drought, etc. Many of the colonists returned to Europe, others to Mobile and neighboring cities; some became men of importance in France, and perhaps the most distinguished, Lefebvre Desnouettes, was lost at sea on his way home. Colonel Raoul kept a ferry near Demopolis, then went to Mexico, returned to France and became Governor of Toulon. Pennier was appointed subagent to the Seminoles, and died in Florida. Clouis kept a tavern in Greensboro and died in Mobile. Chaudron, " the blind poet of the canebrake," who had edited a French paper in Philadelphia and attracted notice by his eulogy of Washington before the Grand Lodge of Masons in that city, died in Mobile in 1846, " leaving many interesting works, which were published in Paris." Clausel lived near Mobile, raising vegetables, which he sold in the city market; returned to France in 1825, became a marshal and was made governor general of Algiers by Louis Philippe. Ravesies was a refugee from St. Domingo, became a business man in Philadelphia, was made agent of the Tombigbee Association in 1820, and after living on his grant moved to Mobile, where he died in 1854.

Daudet in his " Le Brise-Cailloux, 1815," tells a story of a plan to take Napoleon to America, as follows: When, after Waterloo, Napoleon went to the island of Aix, on the eve of his surrender to the English, a ship captain,

Vildieu, proposed to take him to America, through the English lines. Vildieu was an ardent Bonapartist, an excellent sailor, having made a special study of sailing small craft on the open ocean,—was sure of his boat and was ready to take it to the end of the world. The Emperor heard the whole of his story, walked up and down in silence, then looking at the ocean for some minutes, shook his head and said no. The plan did not inspire confidence and he preferred surrendering to the English. Some months later, Vildieu, to show that his plan was a good one, on the same boat that he had offered to Napoleon, sailed to America with two men, one his son. At the end of six weeks, he landed at Halifax, much to the surprise of the crew of a frigate, near which he anchored. Long years afterwards, the son, then an old man, told Daudet the story. How much truth is there in it? At all events it confirms the old tradition that Napoleon really considered this and other projects for taking refuge in the United States.

XV

ROYALIST EXILES

HYDE DE NEUVILLE came to the United States in 1807, a royalist exile, and spent seven years in this country. His first thought was to establish an agricultural settlement, and with this in view he travelled through the country. In his letters (pp. 450, etc., of the first volume of his Memoirs, Paris, 1880) he speaks of the country as he saw it, of the boundless forests, the virgin soil, the industry of the people, of his visits to the Indians in Western New York, of the good work among them of the French missionaries during the rule of France, and their neglect later on; living on the allowance paid by the Holland Land Company, he found them little like the war-like savages described by Chateaubriand. He went as far West as Tennessee, to visit the colonies established by Church and Dupont de Nemours. He corresponded with his countrywomen, Mme. de Noailles, Mme. de Mouchy, Mme. de Damas, Mme. de Rochemore, Mme. de Montechenu, and Mme. de Pastoret, and the Princess de Tremoille. To the last he wrote that if the Americans were wise, they would in time dictate laws to both worlds, the Old and the New, and equal in power the great nations of Europe. He thought thirty or forty years would see this result, and if other Presidents had followed the example of Washington, whom he praises in the strongest terms, perhaps it would not have taken a century to realize his aspirations for the future of American greatness. He formed many strong friendships with the Crugers, the Wilkes, the Churches, the Simonds, the Roulets, and with the Moreaus, the general then in exile from the enmity of Napoleon. Opposed as they had been in politics in France, in America the French exiles met on a common ground of love for France. A brother, after two years of rigorous imprisonment in France, joined him in New York; in the interval he had studied medicine and became in 1810 " Doctor " Neuville. He established in New

York a school for the children of the families exiled in 1800 from St. Domingo. Among them was the family Ricord, whose son, educated in this school, after his return to France became the celebrated Dr. Ricord, and in his house there later on welcomed his benefactor. The State of New York appropriated money for the school and Hyde de Neuville published a monthly literary paper to earn more for it, the *Journal of the Hermit of the Passaic*, for near New Brunswick, New Jersey, he made his home, tried farming, and saw his brother married to the daughter of the Marquis d'Espinville, an exile from Havana. Soon afterwards General Moreau left his peaceful home at Morrisville, Pennsylvania, to return to Europe and fall in battle against France and Napoleon. Hyde de Neuville had opposed the offer made by Moreau to serve with the allies against France. Royalist as he was, Neuville was always a patriotic Frenchman, and frankly wrote to Louis XVIII that he thought Moreau had not taken the right course.

Returning to France at the call of the Duc d'Angoulême, Hyde de Neuville received very flattering letters from Dewitt Clinton, then mayor, later governor, and from the " Economical Society " of New York, for his services as founder and secretary of that useful body. In France and through Europe he resumed all his old activity in support of the royal cause, represented it in the French Legislature after the fall of Napoleon, and in 1816 was sent to the United States as French Minister. Welcomed alike by the public authorities and by his old friends and by the pupils of the school he had founded, after a short stay on his farm at New Brunswick, he went to Washington, where he was warmly received by President Monroe, whose acquaintance he had made when Monroe was American Minister in Paris. He visited Madison and Jefferson at their homes in Virginia, and his correspondence with the Duc de Richelieu, the French Minister of Foreign Affairs (his wife was a Montcalm, another suggestion of France in America), is full of details of their recollections of their stay in Paris as American ministers.

Much of his time was taken up in keeping
179

watch over the French exiles living in the United States. Joseph Bonaparte was the head of a large body of French exiles, busy in scheming for Napoleon. Dupont de Nemours asked help for a very different body of French, refugees from St. Domingo, and Hyde de Neuville gave the French Consuls instructions in regard to them. In New York there were Regnault, Quinet, and Real; in Philadelphia Joseph Bonaparte, Grouchy, Clausel, Garnier de Saintes; in New Orleans, Lefebvre Desnouettes, while a colony was established on the shores of the Ohio. The Duc de Richelieu and the King both approved his sending a portrait of Napoleon, found in the French Legation at Washington, to Joseph Bonaparte, then living at Bordentown, whence it returned later to the legation. Many of the French exiles fled from France to avoid the punishment to which they had been condemned by the Courts for political offences, but the French authorities were apparently only too glad to be rid of them, and the United States gave a peaceful home alike to Girondists and Jacobins, to Royalists and Imperialists, to men of any and of no political opinions, as long as they were peaceful residents and good citizens. While there were some unsuccessful schemes set on foot in the United States to release Napoleon from St. Helena, Neuville wrote home that Grouchy, Lefebvre Desnouettes and Lallemand and Clausel were all loyal to the existing French government. Clausel wrote of the misfortunes of the French officers in exile in the United States, and suggested that help be given them to settle in Havana and Porto Rico. Some of them, however, returned to France and became high officers under the more liberal policy of Louis Philippe. The " Conventionnel Lakanal " was reported by Neuville in 1817, as an agent of Joseph Bonaparte in a plan to make the latter King of Mexico, part of Burr's conspiracy. Just before leaving Washington, to return to France, he obtained from the government there, in 1818, means to continue his " Economical School " in New York, for the children of the impoverished refugees from St. Domingo, and even to help some of them to return to France. He himself went there, and after a short stay in Paris again returned temporarily to Washington, to complete his negotiations with the government of the United States. Finally recalled to France, he found his friends, among them Chateaubriand, in the government, and later on he became a minister of state under Louis Philippe. Living until 1857, he was always fond of dwelling on his American life, as exile, and as minister. His active participation in the relief of his countrymen in exile here was without regard to differences of political opinions, and his name figures with honor in the writings of Chateaubriand and Lamartine, as that of a Frenchman who, both as a private citizen and as a minister, appreciated this country and its welcome.

XVI

Balzac's Story of a French Exile

Balzac in "Les Célibataires, un Ménage de Garçon" (vol. ii of "Scènes de la vie de Province") makes his hero (and a great scamp he is) Captain Philippe Bridau, who went from Saint Cyr in 1813, became a sub-lieutenant in a cavalry regiment, later a lieutenant, for gallantry in saving his colonel in an affair of outpost duty, was made captain at the battle of Fère Champenoise, and ordnance officer by the emperor, got the cross at Montereau; refused to serve under the Bourbons; in 1814 rejoined the emperor at Lyons, accompanied him to the Tuileries, was made chef d'escadron of the Guards Dragoons, wounded at Waterloo, where he gained the cross of the Legion of Honor, was protected by Marshal Davoust, and was put on half pay. After the restoration, he joined General Lallemand in the United States, and coöperated in founding the Champs d'Asile, supported by one of the most curious mystifications known as a national subscription. His mother had given him ten thousand francs on sailing from Havre; no sooner in New York than he drew on her for one thousand francs, having lost everything at Champs d'Asile. Returned to France in 1819, ruined by his misfortunes in Texas and his stay in New York, where speculation and individualism were carried to the highest pitch; where the brutality of interests reached cynicism; where the isolated man looked only for himself; where politeness did not exist,—Bridau, who cared for only one person, himself, became brutal, intemperate, selfish, impolite; misery and suffering had depraved him, New York had taken away his least scruples in morality. Bronzed by his stay in Texas, he had a sharp and short way of making himself respected in New York. The idea of the conquest of Texas by the handful of the imperial army that went there to establish the Champs d'Asile, was a fine one, for in spite of its failure, Texas is a republic full of future greatness. Liberalism under the Restoration was pure egotism; it helped noth-

ing to try to refound the empire in America.
The liberal chiefs soon saw that they were help-
ing Louis XVIII by exporting from France the
glorious remains of its armies, and they abandoned the most devoted, ardent enthusiasts,
who were the first to go.

Bridau was welcomed on his return from
Texas and Champs d'Asile as a " soldier-
laborer." That was the title for a deluge of
engravings, clocks, bronzes, etc., a sort of
tribute to Napoleon and his brave soldiers, who
figured in many plays of the time. It yielded
a fortune, and to this day the " soldier-
laborer " is found in country homes through
France in one or other of these devices.

It was always possible to threaten the
Liberals with the story of the blunders in
Texas, of the waste and pilfering of the
national subscription started for the Champs
d'Asile.

Balzac thus perpetuates the story of the
French " Champs d'Asile " in Texas and its
failure.

XVII

FRENCH MEMBERS OF THE AMERICAN PHILOSOPHICAL SOCIETY

IN 1768 Buffon was elected a member of the American Philosophical Society. This was a genuine tribute to his fame, for in those colonial days the relations of that young society, the outgrowth of Franklin's Junto, were close with the Mother Country. In that year Sir William Johnson and General Gage followed Buffon on its rolls. Mr. T. Penn sent to the secretary, Provost Smith, Maskelyne's Observations on Venus, and he was elected in 1771; Du Simitiere followed, a Frenchman still known by his antiquarian collections, and who no doubt brought some French spirit to the meetings.

In 1772 Le Rey, of the Academy of Sciences in Paris, a friend and correspondent of Franklin, was elected, along with Lieutenant Adye of the Royal Artillery, Lieutenant Hutchins of the Sixtieth (Royal American) Regiment, and Captain John Montresor of the engineers. In 1774 Franklin presented Buffon's works, a gift from the author, and Lavoisier's, with a letter from the author, and queries from Condorcet, and they were elected, along with noteworthy men from London, Barbadoes, and Jamaica,—often in acknowledgment of works presented. In 1775 Franklin, presiding, presented a number of scientific works, and from the outset he was active in thus securing contributions; one of them was an English book, by his friend Sir John Pringle; then followed the interruption of the war, and when meetings were resumed, among the newly-elected members was Gerard de Rayneval, French minister; and a bound volume of the Transactions was presented to him and received with expression of his intention to forward the views of the Society in America and in France; he attended a meeting and agreed to forward to Buffon the thanks of the Society for his superb present of his works. In 1780 Luzerne, the French minister, was elected and attended, and in 1781 Lafayette was elected; at a later meeting Barbé Marbois, recently elected, presided; and " ten pounds of the best kind of raw silk produced in Pennsylvania was ordered to be sent to Lyons, there to be wrought in the most elegant manner, and presented to her Most Christian Majesty as a mark of very high respect." This was following the precedent set in 1770, when the Society for Promoting the Culture of Silk in Pennsylvania sent Franklin a quantity to be presented to the Queen of England and to the Penns, and in 1772, when it sent him forty-five pounds of raw silk, in acknowledgment of the trouble he had taken in the business. In 1783, on the motion of Jefferson, the Philosophical Society ordered that Rittenhouse should make an orrery to be presented to the King of France. In 1784 Vergennes was elected, and later in the year, Lafayette, by special appointment, " entertained the members with an account of the invisible power called Animal Magnetism, lately discovered by Mesmer," and later on Marbois presented the report of the King of France's commissioners on the subject. In 1785 three

volumes of the Proceedings of the Royal
French Academy, and " a very curious elec-
trical apparatus," were presented through Mr.
Marbois, by Dr. Noel of Paris. In 1786 among
the members elected were the Duc de Rochefoucauld, the Marquis de Condorcet, Charles
the aeronaut, Cabanis; in 1787, Otto, French
Minister to the United States, and Cadet de
Vaux; books were received from Belin
de Villeneuve, Moreau de St. Mery, Marbois,
Brissot de Warville; later in the year was
presented Quesnay de Beaurepaire's account
of the Academy of Sciences and Belles Lettres
established by him at Richmond, in Virginia;
Legau was elected in recognition, no doubt,
of his vineyards at Spring Mills, Pennsylvania. In 1791 Duponceau and Ternant,
Minister from France, were elected; in 1792
Mathurin de la Forest and Palisot de Beauvois,
and the latter attended and submitted a paper
on a botanical subject; in 1792 Legau presented his work on Surinam, and later St.
George a paper on the Diseases of St. Domingo
and hot climates in general; and Legau one
on Vine Culture in Pennsylvania. The list of

distinguished Frenchmen who were members of the Philosophical Society was largely increased after France became an ally in the struggle with Great Britain. Many of the Frenchmen who served here were elected, and nearly all of its diplomatic and consular representatives of the time; Lafayette and Chastellux, Otto, and Luzerne, and D'Angeville, and Vergennes; Guichen and Rochefoucauld and Franklin's friends, Le Veillard and Cadet de Vaux, and Cabanis, and Le Roux; in 1789 St. Jean de Crèvecœur (better known as Hector St. John, the name under which he wrote his "Farmer in Pennsylvania"), Moreau de St. Mery, Brissot; in 1791 Gallatin, and Duponceau; in 1793 Valentini; in 1796 Rochefoucauld Liancourt, Grandpré, Le Compte, Adet, French Minister to the United States, Talleyrand Perigord; in 1797 Volney; in 1800 Dupont de Nemours; in 1802 Roume; in 1803 Delambre; in 1806 Destutt de Tracy; in 1807 Lasteyrie; in 1809 Michaux; in 1811 Vauquelin; in 1817 Lesueur, Delametrie, and Deleuze; in 1829 Hyde de Neuville, Pougens, Jomard, and

Remusat. In 1793 money was subscribed towards the expense of Michaux's Western journey of discoveries; Citizen Genet, French Minister, presented a letter and pamphlet on the French reform of the Calendar; and Doctor Nassey addressed the Society in French on botany; later Fauchet, French Minister to the United States, presented a description of the New System of Weights and Measures adopted by the French Republic; M. Lerebours, lately from Paris, gave an account of the late curious and useful discoveries and inventions relating to the arts, made in France since the commencement of the Revolution, with a number of pamphlets on the same subject; in 1795 Moreau de St. Mery presented some curious articles from St. Domingo and a medal of Louis XVI, July 17, 1789, and later a silver medal of Louis XV, struck on the occasion of the peace of 1763; he seems to have been a pretty steady attendant at the meetings. In 1796 Doctor Grassi, " late of Bordeaux, now of Philadelphia," Rochefoucauld Liancourt, Le Comte, Le Fessier de Grandpré, and Citizen Adet, Minister Plenipotentiary of the French Republic to the United States, were elected at the same meeting, and Grassi, Adet, and Liancourt attended several subsequent meetings; later Lerebours, " late of Paris, now of Philadelphia," Larocque, and M. Talleyrand Perigord were present; in 1797 Volney attended meetings; he was present when St. Mery presented " from the author," Adet's " Doctrine of Phlogistique and the Decomposition of Water " in French; then, in 1800, the Society received Dupont de Nemours' book, " Philosophie de l'Univers," and thanks were voted and delivered by Jefferson; and later more papers were received from Dupont, yet the committee to which one of them was referred, reported that although ingenious, it was not of sufficient importance to publish, but later on the publication was ordered of his translation of Baudry de Loziere's paper on Animal Cotton.

In 1803 the National Institute of France promised, as successors of the French Academy, to resume correspondence and exchanges; General Toussard presented a paper on proving cannon; the library was enriched by the numerous volumes of " L'Encyclopedie." In 1805 Dupont de Nemours sent from Paris De Candolle's " Essai sur les propriétés médicinales des plantes," and many French books were received from other sources, some by purchase, many as gifts, from Hassler the volumes necessary to complete the Transactions of the French Academy of Science, which Franklin left to it.

It is a noteworthy fact that Franklin's legacy to the Philosophical Society was ninety-one volumes of the History of the Royal Academy of Sciences of France, and that later the Society bought from Franklin's library many of his French scientific works, *e.g.*, Bailly's History of Astronomy, those of Condamine, De Luc, Desaguliér, Berthelot, De Saussure, Lavoisier, De la Lande, as well as a number of serial volumes of French scientific societies. Thus was begun that collection of the Transactions, etc., of French scientific societies that now form so important a part of the library.

In 1807 Jefferson presented pamphlets from the authors, De Lasteyrie on Cotton and Cossigny on Sugar. In 1809 Michaux obtained the completion to date of the French scientific journals, and imported for the Society the works of Brongniart, Bronchart, Hauy, and Berthelot. In 1817 the election of Lesueur brought a French naturalist who made frequent communication of his researches; he was constant in attendance at the meetings, and took part in the election of Desmarest, Blainville, and Latreille of Paris in 1819; he served diligently both before and after his Western visit with Maclure; in 1823 he was present when the Society elected Joseph Count de Survilliers and Lucien Prince of Canino. In 1824 Lafayette was received by the Society with marked honors. In 1825 Charles Bonaparte attended and he and Lesueur and Duponceau recalled the days of frequent attendance by French members and visitors. Charles Bonaparte made donations to the library, and Lesueur gave his drawings from the fossil bones in the cabinet. In 1829 Hyde de Neuville, then French Minister to the United States, was elected a member; and Pougens; in 1830 M. A. Julien; in 1831 Louis Philippe, King of the French; in 1833 the members of the Society subscribed towards a statue of Cuvier, and sent the money in the name of the Society to the French Academy; in 1833 M. Nicollet " of Paris, then in Georgia," reported his progress in scientific observations in the Southern States; in 1834 the death of Lafayette was formally announced and due action taken. In 1837 the death of Barbé Marbois in his ninety-fifth year was announced and Duponceau was appointed to prepare a memoir of him. He had been Napoleon's Minister of Finance. Other notable Frenchmen elected were Larrey, the great French surgeon, Roux de Rochelle, Guizot, De Tocqueville, Poussin, the French Minister to the United States, Pouchet, Michel Chevalier, Cauchey, Brown-Sequard, Durand, Elie de Beaumont, Milne-Edwards, St. Claire-Deville, J. B. Dumas, Verneuil, Lesquereux, Renan, Boucher des Perthes, Gasparin, De Rongé, Linant, Mariette, Lartet, Carlier, Leon Say, Broca, Viollet le Duc, Claude Jannet, Paul Leroy Beaulieu, Rosny, Pasteur, Hovelacque, Levasseur, Duruy, Nadaillac, Reville, Topinard, Taine, Berthelot, George Bertin, Delambre, Delage, Becquerel, Darboux, Maspero, Poincare. Thus from the early election of Buffon, with the later welcome to the French who served in the American war, the hearty reception of French refugees and exiles, down to our own day, with its representatives of French science and letters, the records of the Society show how largely its membership was recruited by notable Frenchmen. At the election of 1907, the Society chose M. Jusserand, the French ambassador to the United States, and a scholarly man of letters.

Pontgibaud says that " Duportail told him the French refugees found Philadelphia an ark of safety. Constitutionalists, Conventionalists, Thermidorians, Fructidorians, as well as Royalists and Girondists, met on common ground; Moreau de St. Mery kept a stationer's shop, where they met to discuss the future of France; Noailles, Liancourt, Talleyrand speculated in stocks and land; the French cook who supplied the Duc d'Orleans and his brothers, forbade Volney coming to his little restaurant while they were there."

In 1844 Doctor Dunglison delivered an eulogium on Duponceau. It followed in due course that on Franklin by Provost Smith, that on Rittenhouse by Doctor Rush, that on Doctor Wistar by Chief Justice Tilghman, that on Tilghman by Duponceau, and that on Jefferson by Nicholas Biddle. Born on the west coast of France in 1760, Duponceau learned English from the soldiers of an Irish regiment stationed in the town, and later Italian in the same way. Unwillingly he took the tonsure, but soon gave up holy orders, and went to Paris to seek his fortune. Through Beaumarchais he entered the service of Steuben as secretary, and with him landed in Portsmouth, New Hampshire, in 1777. As a captain of infantry of the line of the Army of the Revolution he received a pension until the day of his death. After leaving the army, in 1781, owing to ill health, he became a citizen of Pennsylvania, and settled in Philadelphia. He was secretary of Robert R. Livingston, Secretary for Foreign Affairs, studied law and was admitted to the bar in 1785, and became one of its acknowledged leaders. In 1827 he was elected a member of the French Institute, in recognition of his linguistic studies, and in 1835 was awarded the prize founded by Volney, for his Memoir on the Indian languages of North America. He spent time and money in an unsuccessful effort to introduce the production and manufacture of silk in this country. Elected to the Philosophical Society in 1791, he became a vice-president in 1816, and president in 1827. Among his bequests to the Society were twenty-one volumes of the *Moniteur* from 1789 to 1809.

Talleyrand read a " Memoir concerning the Commercial Relations of the United States with England," at the National Institute, the 15th Germinal, in the Year V, to which was added " An Essay upon the Advantages to be derived from New Colonies in the existing circumstances," read at the Institute, the 15th Messidor in the Year V, with Notes, in the month of Ventôse, Year VII,—published in London for Longman, 1806, in a pamphlet of 87 pages. In it there are a good many references to his visit here. " In every part of America through which I have travelled, I did not meet a single Frenchman who did not find himself a stranger. It is a novel sight to the traveller, who, setting out from a principal city, where society is in perfection, passes in succession through all the degrees of civilization and industry, which he finds constantly growing weaker and weaker, until in a few days, he arrives at misshapen and rude cabins, formed of the trunks of trees lately cut down. It would require a French establishment in America to counteract the indolence and want of native character.

" Have we not seen of late years, since there have been political opinions in France, men of all parties embark together, and go to run the same risks upon the uninhabited banks of the Scioto?

" Louisiana remains French, although it has been under the domination of the Spaniards for more than thirty years, and in Canada, although in the power of the English for the same length of time, the colonists of these two countries were Frenchmen, they are so still."

In Mr. Whitelaw Reid's introduction to the Duc de Broglie's edition of the Memoirs of Talleyrand, (there could not be better sponsors to their authenticity, in spite of the suspicion thrown on them by the fact that M. de Bacourt was their custodian,) he says: " Talleyrand spent many months in the United States soon after the establishment of their independence, in which France had aided; and while a Revolution, stimulated in part by the American example, was in progress in his own land, he found in his recollections of his American visit almost nothing suggested by either event, and nothing concerning the great man, then Chief Magistrate of the country which gave him hospitality. His lack of sympathy with republicanism, whether in the United States or in France, explains the one omission; and Washington's refusal to receive him, explains the other. Lord Lansdowne had given him a warm letter of introduction to Washington, setting forth that Talleyrand was really in exile because, although a bishop, he had desired to promote the general freedom of worship, and eulogizing him for having sacrificed his ambition in the Church to his devotion to principle. Washington possibly had his own views as to the extent to which Talleyrand's exile was due to his high religious principles. Hamilton's influence, always great, was joined to Lord Lansdowne's eulogy, but both were unavailing. The refusal to receive the French exile, however, was quietly put upon political grounds." Following his expulsion from England by Pitt, Talleyrand naturally had little praise for either Pitt or Washington. Of his later dealings with the United States, Mr. Reid says: " Talleyrand gave notice to the American Ministers Plenipotentiary in Paris that they must buy peace or leave the country. When the American Commissioners resented his demand for a bribe of two hundred and fifty thousand dollars for himself and a bigger one called a loan for the Directory, his representative naively said, ' Don't you know that everything is bought in Paris? Do you dream that you can get on with this government without paying your way?' This from the man who had been honored with Hamilton's friendship, and who shrewdly said, shortly after the adoption of the Constitution, ' that was the true date of the foundation of the United States; it was the real sheet-anchor of American independence,' was a cynical measure of the men in office under it."

In his story figure the names of his fellow-exiles, men of a very different type, Noailles, who fell in action near Havana fighting for France, Brissot de Warville, who died on the scaffold, Barbé Marbois, French Consul in Philadelphia, and others.

In his narrative he tells the story of meeting Benedict Arnold, just as Talleyrand was leaving for America, and in vain asking him for letters of introduction to his friends in America, and Arnold's characteristic reply: " I am the only American who cannot give you letters for his own country." In Philadelphia he met Casanove and Huidekoper, agents of the Holland Land Company, and travelled with the latter inland. He could not have had a better guide. He speaks of the two winters spent in Philadelphia and New York, and praises Hamilton as on a par with Pitt or Fox or other distinguished European statesmen. He speaks in high praise of the enterprise of American merchants and says that in 1794 he witnessed the return of the first American trading expedition to the East Indies, and in the following year fourteen American vessels started for India from different ports in order to obtain a share of the enormous profits secured by the English company. He spent thirty months in the United States, keeping up close correspondence with Mme. de Staël, to whom on his return he owed his introduction to Barras, and through him his relations with Napoleon. It was before the National Institute, organized in 1795, on the foundation of the old academies abolished in 1792, to which he was elected a member of the section of Moral and Political Sciences, that he read his paper on " The Commercial Intercourse of England with the United States," published in its volume of Proceedings of 1799, along with a second, on " Advantages to be Derived from New Colonies," which he says, attracted a certain notice. These are the results of his stay in the United States, and have value and interest on that account.

In the collection of the Philosophical Society there is a MS. of Mr. Samuel Breck, dated 1862, giving an account of the early members of the Society he had known; Mr. Breck was then in his ninety-first year. He was born in 1771 in Boston; he had become a member of the Society in 1838, and died in 1862, shortly after writing, at the request of Doctor Bache, then president of the Society, his memoranda. They have the personal note of actual acquaintance with those whose names are now historical and of others who by their writings have an interest as members of this venerable Society. He says: " Talleyrand came to Philadelphia in 1794 to reside there until France is at peace. He took the oath of allegiance to the State of Pennsylvania. He listened to Hamilton's argument in the United States Court on the constitutionality of the Carriage Tax law. He equipped himself in full hunting-suit for a visit to the then Western frontier, and saw there only the destruction of the forests, just as in our hardy fishermen he saw only idlers. Yet both sea and forest were then beginning to earn sums that laid the foundation of our wealth.

" Volney was another refugee from the violence of the French Revolution. He taught French to a few pupils whose liberal pay contributed to his support; he made an offer of marriage, which was rejected. Perhaps this accounted, in part at least, for his haughty and morose nature, jealous of the least appearance of slight or neglect; and presuming much upon his celebrity as a writer, he judged Americans in his conversations and publications as an inferior people, unworthy of renown and wanting in morals and republican purity. Washington, in his opinion, would never have been more than a colonel in the French army; he condemned the growing luxury in America, and anticipated a visit of the Algerine pirates to levy tribute on our ports.

" Brissot de Warville was equally hostile to the growing luxury and refinement of the cities of America, as a sign of decay of republican simplicity. Alike they condemned American manners, climate, food, and both longed for the return to France and to the honors awaiting them. Brissot, however, was guillotined in 1793.

" Rochefoucauld Liancourt took his exile and

poverty in very good spirits, and his account of his travels is kindly towards the New World.

"Louis Philippe came to Philadelphia in 1796, and bore his enforced exile good-naturedly. He painted a miniature of Miss Willing and was said to have asked her to marry him. He was joined in Philadelphia by his younger brothers, the Ducs de Montpensier and Beaujolais. They made a journey on horseback through Pennsylvania and New York and to the Falls of Niagara."

Mr. Breck mentions the fact that Gouverneur Morris secured for Mrs. Robert Morris an annuity of sixteen hundred dollars out of the lands bought by Le Ray de Chaumont, and this was her sole support until her death.

Mr. Breck spent four years at a military school at Loreze in the south of France, and in 1787 on his arrival in Paris on his way home to America made the acquaintance of Hector St. John de Crèvecœur, the author of the "Letters from an American Farmer," which did much to enlist foreign interest in America. His book, published in Paris in 1787, covers his personal experiences as a farmer in Pennsylvania from 1770 to 1786. Through him Breck made the acquaintance of Brissot de Warville, who later took refuge from the French Revolution in Philadelphia, and returned American hospitality by violent diatribes against American morals and manners. "Brissot came in 1788 and had little good to say in his book, published on his return to France, as to our future. Chastellux, on the other hand, found only good to say of the people and the country whose independence he as an officer of Rochambeau's army had helped to secure; his 'Travels in the United States' are of value and interest as a contemporary record of the country. His tribute to Washington is still often quoted, for it gives a clear and vivid picture of the great American, as Chastellux saw and knew him, both in war and in peace. Chastellux was elected a member of the Philosophical Society in 1781, and died a field marshal in 1788."

Breck's Recollections, published in Philadelphia in 1877, give a further picture of the time. "In Philadelphia all the distinguished emigrants from France took up their abode,—

Talleyrand, his companion, Beaumais, Vicomte de Noailles, the Duc de Rochefoucauld Liancourt, Volney, and subsequently Louis Philippe and his brothers, the Ducs de Montpensier and Beaujolais, and later General Moreau. Talleyrand and his companion, Beaumais, equipped themselves in the costume of backwoodsmen, with rifles, guns, and hunting-shirts, for their Western tour. Volney was a timid, peevish, sour-tempered man. Washington hated free-thinkers and as President declined to notice the French emigrants, and to get rid of Volney, on his request at Mount Vernon for a circular letter of introduction, gave him one that Volney thought too feeble for his exalted merit, hence the manner in which he speaks of that great man. De Noailles had been in America with Rochambeau; his sister was the wife of Lafayette. His form was perfect—a fine face, tall, graceful, the first amateur dancer of the age, and of very pleasing manners. He became a trader and speculator,—every day at the coffee-house or exchange, busy, holding his bank book in one hand and a broker or merchant with the other, while he drove his bargains."

Among the scientific men brought to this country in 1827 by William Maclure, to help out his plan of a geological survey of the United States, were a number of Frenchmen. One of them was Charles Lesueur, a French naturalist and draughtsman, who drew some of the engravings for Say's Conchology, had been employed in the Jardin des Plantes of Paris, sent to it many reports of his American explorations, and contributed papers to the American Philosophical Society and to the Academy of Natural Sciences, of both of which he was an active member. He taught in the scientific school founded at New Harmony, Indiana, of which Maclure was part founder with Robert Owen; later he returned to Philadelphia, where he gave lessons in drawing and painting, and continued his scientific researches; these were rewarded by appointment as Director of the Museum of Natural History of Havre, his native city, and he died there soon after his return to France. A sympathetic memoir of

14

him was recently printed by the Society of Americanists of Paris.

Another of Maclure's scientific corps was Phignepul d'Arusmont, and still another, Mme. Frétageot. Under them a large school was established, on Owen's plan of teaching both useful arts and mathematics and natural history, Lesueur taking an active part in the work. For many years New Harmony remained the chief scientific and educational centre in the West, influencing the country and the people in many ways, largely owing to the presence there of Frenchmen of science and their instruction.

Appendix A

Bibliography

Jeffreys: History of the French Dominions in America. London, 1761; folio.

D'Anville: Mémoires pour la Carte intitulée: Canada, Louisiane, etc. Paris, 1756; 4°.

Lescarbot: Histoire de la Nouvelle France. Paris, 1618.

Dussieux: La Canada sous la domination française. Paris, 1862.

Poussin: La puissance Américaine. Paris, 1848.

Lozére: Histoire des États Unis. Paris, 1845.

Carlier: Histoire du peuple Américain. Paris, 1864.*

Tocqueville: La Democratie en Amérique. Paris, 1838-40.

Laboulaye: Histoire politique des États Unis. Paris, 1855.

Le Page du Pratz: Hist. de la Louisiane. Paris, 1758.

---

* An answer to the work of Tocqueville.

APPENDIX A

Vergennes: Mém. Hist. et polit. sur la Louisiane. Paris, 1802.

Milfort: Voyages dans la Louisiane. Paris, 1802.

Barbe Marbois: Hist. de la Louisiane. Paris, 1829.

Monette: History of the Discovery and Settlement of the Valley of the Mississippi; 7 vols. New York, 1846.

Chotteau: Les Français en Amérique (1775-83). Paris, 1876.

Gaffarel: Hist. de la Floride française. Paris, 1876.

Rameau: La colonie canadienne de Detroit. Paris, 1881.

Maze: Rôle de la France dans la République des États Unis. Paris, 1879.

Margry: Découvertes et Establissements des Français dans l'ouest et dans le sud de l'Amérique septentrionale. 1614-1754; 6 vols. Paris, 1888.

Brissot de Warville: New Travels in the United States, 1788. Translated by Chas. Brockden Brown. Philadelphia, 1804.

Volney's Travels in the United States: Translated "by his friend" Chas. Brockden Brown. Philadelphia, 1804.

Perrin du Lac: Voyage dans les deux Louisianes. Lyon, 1801.

APPENDIX A

Vicomte de Noailles: Marins et soldats Français en Amérique pendant la Guerre de l'Indépendance des États Unis (1778–1783). Paris, Perrin, 1893.

Quesnay de Beaurepaire: Virginia Historical Society, vol. ii, N. S., by R. H. Gains; pp. 166, etc.

Love and Adventures of M. [Louis Lebeau] Du Portail, late Major-General in the Armies of the United States, with incidents of the late Count Pulauski. Boston, 1799; New Haven, 1813.

The French Régime in Wisconsin, 1634-1748. Wisconsin State Historical Society, vols. 16 and 17, 1902 and 1906.

Chevalier, Michel: Lettres sur l'Amérique du Nord. Paris, 1836.

Franche, Gabriel: Narrative of a Voyage to the Northwest Coast of America in the Years 1811-12-13-14. Translated by J. V. Huntingdon. New York, 1854.

Beaujour, Felix de: Sketch of the United States from 1800 to 1810, with statistical tables. Translated from the French by William Walton. London, 1814.

Bossu: Travels through Louisiana. Translated from the French by John Reinhold Forster. London, 1771.

De Fonpertuis: Les États Unis. Paris, 1854.

APPENDIX A

Brissot, de Warville, J. P.: Nouveau voyage dans les États Unis fait en 1788; 3 vols. Paris, 1791.

Id.: Translation, with his Life; 2 vols. London, 1794.

Chastellux: Travels in North America, 1780–1–2; 2 vols. Paris, 1785; 1788; London, 1787.

Id.: Examen Critique par J. P. Brissot de Warville. Philadelphia, 1788.

Collot, Gen. Victor: A Journey in North America. Paris, 1826.

Michaux, F. A.: Travels to the Westward of the Allegheny Mountains, etc. Translated by B. Lambert. London, 1805.

Robin, C. C.: Voyages dans la Louisiane, 1802-6; 3 vols. Paris, 1807.

Id.: New Travels in North America, exhibiting the campaigns of the allied armies, etc. Philadelphia, 1783.

St. John, J. Hector: Lettres d'un fermier de Pennsylvanie, traduites de l'Anglais. Amsterdam, 1769.

Id.: Letters from an American Farmer. London, 1782; Philadelphia, 1793.

Volney, C. F.: Tableau du climat et sol des États Unis, suivi d'eclaircissemens sur la Floride et sur la colonie Française au Scioto; 2 vols. Paris, 1802.

Id.: Translation. London, 1804.

APPENDIX A

Rochefoucauld Liancourt, Duke de: Travels through the United States, 1795-6-7; 2 vols. London, 1799.

Puisaye: Mémoires, London, 1803-8; 7 vols. [A collection of his Papers in the British Museum.]

Brown, Chas. Brockden: Address to the Government of the United States on the Cession of Louisiana. Philadelphia, 1803.
Id.: Literary Magazine and American Register. Philadelphia, 1803-7.
Id.: American Register. Philadelphia, 1806-9.

Brissot de Warville: Commerce of America with Europe, particularly with France and Great Britain, comparatively stated and explained, showing the importance of the American Revolution to the Interests of France, and pointing out the actual situation of the United States in regard to Trade, Manufactures and Population. By J. P. Brissot de Warville and Etienne Clairère. Translated from the last French edition, revised by Brissot, and called the second volume of his View of America, with the Life of Brissot, and an Appendix by the Translator [Joel Barlow]. London, 1794; New York, 1795.

Bortel Dumont: Voyage à la Louisiane dans les années 1794-8. Paris, An. IX.

APPENDIX A

Brissot de Warville: * New Travels in the United
States Performed in 1788. London, 1792;
New York, 1792; Boston, 1797.
New Travels in the United States, etc.; 2
vols. London, 1794.
Crèvecœur: Voyage dans la haute Penn.; 3 vols.
Paris, 1801.
Crèvecœur: Lettres d'un cultivateur Américain.
Paris, 1784, 2 vols.; 1787, 3 vols.
Drouin de Bercy: L'Europe et l'Amérique. Paris,
1818.

---

* Sabin's Note s. v. Brissot: The author came to the
United States just before the French Revolution, for
the purpose of selecting a suitable place for establishing a colony of respectable persons, who had deter-
mined to abandon the then despotic government of
France and seek an asylum under the mild and equal
government of the United States. M. Brissot was
commissioned to collect every necessary information,
prior to the execution of so important a plan. These
volumes contain the results of his assiduous labors and
minute enquiries, and sufficiently manifest that he was
qualified to accomplish such an arduous undertaking.
The second volume is a new edition of Brissot and
Clairère's De la France et des Etats Unis, etc., printed
at Paris in 1787, and in English in 1788. A German
translation by J. R. Foster was printed in Berlin in
1792, and another in Hof in three volumes in 1796; a
Dutch translation in Amsterdam in 1794 in two volumes.
It was also published by Brisson in Paris in three
volumes in 1791, and in a German translation by
Ehrmann in Heidelberg in 1792.

APPENDIX A

Perrin du Lac: Voyage dans les deux Louisianes. Paris, 1805.

Robin, l'Abbé: Nouveau Voyage dans l'Amérique septentrionale en l'année 1781, etc. Philadelphia and Paris, 1782.

Bayard: Voyage dans l'intérieur des États Unis pendant l'été de 1791. Paris, 1819.

Mably: Observations sur le gouvernement et les lois des États Unis. Amsterdam, 1784.

Mazzei: Recherches sur les États Unis, etc.; 4 vols. Colle, 1788.

Chateaubriand: Voyages en Amérique. Brussels, 1828.

Le Page du Pratz: Hist. de la Louisiane; 3 vols.

De Pauw: Recherches sur les Américains; 2 vols. London, 1770-1.

L'Académie des Sciences et Beaux Arts des États Unis de l'Amérique, Richmond, Va.: Mémoire et prospectus, concernant l'Académie etablie à Richemond, capitale de la Virginie; par le Chevalier Quesnay de Beaurepaire, Fondateur, Président. Paris, Cailleau, Imprimeur de l'Académie de Richmond, 1788; 8 p. l., 52 pp., 8°.

Murat Achille: Esquisse morale et politique sur les États Unis. Paris, 1832.

Bossu: Nouveau Voyage, etc. Amsterdam, 1778.

APPENDIX A

Raynal: Tableau et révolutions des Colonies Anglaises, etc. Amsterdam, 1781.

Bulletin of the New York Public Library, March, 1907.

Laval, Antoine Jean de: Voyage de la Louisiana, fait par Ordre du Roy en l'année mil sept cent vingt: Dans lequel sont traitées diverses matieres de Phisique, Astronomie, Geographie et Marine. Divers Voyages faits pour la correction de la Carte de la Cote de Province; Et des Reflexions sur quelques points du Sisteme de M. Newton. Par le P. Laval, de la Compagnie de Jesus. " A valuable and scientific book of travels, which enters very fully into the Physical Geography, etc., of the French dominions in Louisiana and the valley of the Mississippi." Maps, folding tables, etc. Paris, 1728, 4°.

Selections from the Gallipolis Papers, arranged and edited by Theodore T. Belote. Quarterly Publication of the Historical and Philosophical Society of Ohio, vol. ii, 1907, No. 2. Cincinnati, Ohio.

The Scioto Speculation and the French Settlement, by Theodore T. Belote, University of Cincinnati. Cincinnati, Ohio.

Appendix B

FRENCH PLACE NAMES IN THE UNITED
STATES [1]

Abbeville: South Carolina; settled by French.

Alexandria: New York; after Alexander Le Ray,
son of J. D., who fell in a duel in 1836.

Atala: Mississippi; after Chateaubriand's
heroine.

Bienville: Louisiana; after the French explorer.

Bonaparte: New York and Alabama.

Bonneville: Nevada and New York.

Bonpland: California.

Bordeaux: South Carolina.

Bourbon: Kentucky, Indiana and Kansas.

Cadillac: Michigan.

Cape Vincent: New York; after son of Le Ray
de Chaumont.

Carondelet: Louisiana.

Castine: Maine.

Champaign: Ohio and Illinois.

---

[1] Place Names in the United States, by Henry Gannett, U. S. Geol. Survey Bulletin No. 258. Washington, D. C.

APPENDIX B

Charlevoix: Michigan.

Chateaugay: New York.

Chaumont: New York.

Choteau: Montana and South Dakota.

Creve Cœur: Missouri.

Des Moines: Iowa.

Duluth: Minnesota.

Faribault: Minnesota:

Gallia: Ohio; settled by a French colony, 1790.

Gallipolis: Ohio; settled by a French colony, 1790.

Havre de Grace: Maryland; from the French port.

Hennepin: Illinois and Minnesota.

Hugoton (for Victor Hugo): Kansas, and

Hugo: Colorado.

Iberville: Louisiana.

Isle Lamotte: Vermont.

Joliet: Illinois.

Labaddie: Missouri.

Laclede: Missouri (founder of St. Louis).

Lafayette: Arkansas, Florida, Louisiana, Mississippi, Maryland, New Hampshire, Ohio, Wisconsin.*

Lagrange: (after Lafayette's country home): Indiana, New York, North Carolina.

---

*For a number of other Lafayettes see U. S. Postal Guide.

APPENDIX B

La Harpe: Illinois (after French explorer).

Lahonte: New York.

Lamartine: Wisconsin.

La Motte: New York (after French soldier).

Lamy: New Mexico (after Archbishop Lamy).

Langlade: Wisconsin (after first white settler).

Laporte: Pennsylvania (after early French settler).

Laramie: Ohio (after early French Canadian trader).

Lasalle: Illinois, New York, Texas.

Lavallette: New Jersey.

Le Claire: Iowa.

Le Ray: New York.

Le Raysville: Pennsylvania.

Lesueur: Minnesota (after early explorer).

Low Freight: Arkansas (tr. of " l'eau froid ").

Luzerne: Pennsylvania (after French Minister).

Maine: (after estate of Henrietta Maria, Queen of France).

Mandeville: Louisiana (after early French owner).

Marengo: Alabama, Illinois, Iowa.

Marietta: Ohio (after Marie Antoinette), Pennsylvania.

Marseilles: Illinois.

Massac: Illinois (after French Minister of Marine during French and Indian wars).

Massena: New York.

APPENDIX B

Massilon: Ohio.

Maurepas: Louisiana.

Marmiton: Missouri (from French word for scullion).

Meredosia: Illinois (from marais d'osier).

Montcalm: Michigan.

Napoleon: Ohio.

New Orleans: Louisiana.

New Rochelle: New York.

Nicollet: Minnesota.

Orleans: Louisiana, Nebraska, New York and Virginia.

Papillion: Nebraska.

Papinsville: Mississippi (after Pierre Mellecourt Papin).

Paris: New York, Kentucky, Maine.

Père Marquette: Michigan.

Pierre: Dakota (after P. Choteau).

Plaquemines: Louisiana (named by Bienville on account of persimmons).

Pomme de Terre: Missouri.

Poteau: Arkansas.

Prairie du Chien: Wisconsin.

Prairie du Rocher: Illinois.

Prairie du Sac: Wisconsin.

Presque Isle: Maine and Michigan.

Purgatoire Rivière: Arkansas, Colorado.

Quebec (quel bec): Canada.

Rapides: Louisiana.

Roche Percée: Missouri.

Roche Moutonnée: Colorado.

Rochelle: Illinois.

Roche à Gris: Wisconsin.

Roseau: Minnesota.

Sabine: Louisiana (French for cypress).

Saint Anne: Illinois.

Saint Anthony: Minnesota.

Saint Augustine: Florida.

Saint Bernard: Louisiana.

Saint Charles: Louisiana, Missouri.

Saint Clair: Michigan, Alabama, Missouri, Illinois, Nebraska, Pennsylvania.

Saint Cloud: Minnesota.

Saint Croix: Maine, Minnesota, Wisconsin.

Saint François: Missouri.

Saint Genevieve: Missouri.

Saint Helena: Louisiana and Colorado.

Saint Ignace: Michigan.

Saint James: Louisiana.

Saint Johnsbury: Vermont (after St. John de Crevecœur).

Saint Joseph; Michigan, Missouri.

Saint Landry: Louisiana.

Saint Louis: Missouri, Minnesota.

Saint Martin: Louisiana.

Sans Tache: California.

Sault Ste. Marie: Michigan.

Tchemanahaut (chemin en haut): Arkansas.

APPENDIX B

Terre Haute: Indiana.

Terrebonne: Louisiana.

Terre Noir: Arkansas.

Theresa: New York (after daughter of Le Ray de Chaumont).

Thibodaux: Louisiana.

Toulon: Tennessee and Illinois.

Trempealeau (trempe à l'eau): Wisconsin.

Vergennes: Vermont.

Versailles: Indiana and eight other places.

Wolf River (rivière de loup): Kansas.

Index

Acadians.................................... 39
Adams, Herbert B............................ 73
Adet................................83, 190, 192
Alabama.....................................15, 159
Allegheny, the...............................18, 116
American Catholic Historical Society, the 86
American Philosophical Society, the, 8, 82, 139, 186
    190, 193–196, 198, 203, 209
Armand, Colonel.........................64, 78, 79
Autichamp, D'................................ 72
Ayrault..................................... 55
Baird..............................9, 32, 52, 55
Balch....................................... 68
Balzac...............................160, 183, 185
Bancroft...........................7, 13 note, 15
Baratarians................................50, 51
Barbé Marbois...................42, 188, 195, 202
Bardstown, Kentucky..........................97–98
Barlow, Joel................................. 20
Bartram..................................... 79
Bastrop, Baron de........................... 45, 48
Bayards, the................................ 58
Beaujolais, Duc de...........................208
Beaujour, Felix de........................... 82
Beaulieu, Pierre Leroy.......................11, 146
Beaurepaire, Quesnay de.............73, 74, 76, 189
Belle Riviere................................ 18
Benevolent Society, the French................. 87

225

INDEX

Bernadotte...................................32, 40
Bernard....................................... 73
Berthier...................................40, 65
Bienville, Celeron de...............16, 18, 25, 36, 37
Boisbriant, Pierre Dugue.......................... 23
Bonaparte, Charles............................194
——— General.............................41, 80
——— Joseph ...109, 160, 162–165, 166–168, 180, 181
——— Lucien..................................... 40
Bonneville.................................65, 66
Boré...39, 49
Bouvier, John.................................... 88
Bowdoin.. 54
Bourbon, county, Kentucky...................78, 98
Breck, Samuel........................203, 206, 207
Bridau.....................................184, 185
Brillat Savarin..............................103–105
Brissot de Warville.............82, 189, 202, 205, 207
Burr, Aaron..................................... 48
Cabet............................154, 156, 157, 169
Cadillac.....................................13, 33, 37
Cahokia.........17, 22, 23, 25–27, 43, 97, 98, 132, 138
Carolana... 14
Carondelet...................................46–48
"Cartier to Frontenac" (Winsor)................. 32
Casgrain, L'Abbé............................... 38
Castine, Maine................................... 33
Champlain...................................... 17
Champs d'Asile...................160, 167, 183–185
Charleston, South Carolina..................... 54
"Charleston" (Mrs. St. Julien Ravenel)........91 note
Charlevoix....................................37, 39
Chartres, Fort 23, 25, 38, 43
Chastellux............................65, 71, 190, 207
Chateaubriand...............78–80, 82, 99, 176, 182

226

INDEX

Chatelet, Du............................ 17
Chaudron............................159
Chaumont, Le Ray de.............106, 108, 163, 206
Cheverus, Archbishop......................... 89
Choiseul........................16, 17, 95, 96
Chouteau.............................. 43
——— Family, the........................ 45
Cibot, Father............................ 86
Cincinnati, Society of the.................... 67
Clark, George Rogers, ...19, 27, 29–31, 85
——— Lewis and........................ 45
Clausel 159, 174, 181
Collot........................26, 31, 48, 83
Coudray, Du............................ 69
Coxe.................................. 14
Crèvecœur, Fort........................ 25
——— Hector St. John de...................206
Crozat................................ 37
Cutler, Manasseh.......................29, 135
Damas................................ 71
Decrès 41, 42
Delaware, Country, Upper...................60–62
Depauw..............................139
Desert, Mount.........................33, 34
Des Moines River........................ 22
Detroit.......................13, 17, 22, 33
De Turk, Isaac.......................... 58
Dumas................................ 65
Dumont................................ 38
Du Lac, Perrin.......................... 46
Dupetit Thouars...........69, 141, 143, 145, 146, 148
Duponceau.........................134, 197
Du Pont de Nemours, Pierre Samuel, 58, 121, 176
    180, 190, 193
Du Ponts, the.......................... 58

INDEX

Duportail...................................196
Du Pratz, Le Page............................ 47
Dupuy, Nicholas.............................. 61
Dupuys, the................................. 54
Durocher.................................... 45
Du Simitiere................................186
"Early Exploration of Louisiana, The" (Cox)...... 45
Explorers, early French...................... 17
Faneuil..................................... 54
Fauchet.....................................191
Ferree, Mme................................. 57
Fersen, Count............................... 64
Fiske....................................... 33
Fortier..................................42, 43
"French Agricultural and Manufacturing Society,
    The,"...................................161
French Creek................................ 18
"French in America, The" (Balch).............. 68
French Grant, the.....................21, 31, 133
French Patriotic Society, the................. 77
"Frontenac" (Parkman)........................ 33
Galissoniere................................ 18
Gallia County...............................135
Gallipolis, 19, 31, 46, 84, 98, 99, 125, 131, 132–134
    135, 136, 137, 139
Galvez 39
Gayarré..................................48, 51
Genet................................30, 31, 48, 191
Gratiot..................................... 26
Great Kanawha, the........................18, 20
Great Miami, the............................ 18
Gregoires, the.............................. 33
Grouchy....................................160
Harmar, Fort................................ 29
Harmar, General............................. 28

INDEX

Henry, Patrick.................................. 29
"Historical and Political Essays"(Lodge)......... 10
Historical Society, American Catholic............ 86
"History of Louisiana, A" (Fortier)............. 35
Holland Land Company, the.....................176
Hourie..139
Huger.....................................93, 95
Huguenots, the...........10, 11, 52–57, 59, 91, 92, 93
"Huguenot Emigration to America" (Baird) 32, 57
Huguenot Society of New York, the. ....56 note
"History of the Huguenots" (Baird).............. 9
Humbert, General............................44, 51
Hyde de Neuville, 162, 165, 166, 167, 176, 178, 180, 194
Iberville, D' 13, 36, 47
Icarians............................152, 154, 155, 169
Illinois..................10, 17, 22, 23, 25, 26, 45, 85
Illinois, the. 28, 29
Indiana.. 17
Indies, Company of the........................ 37
Inquisition, Holy 46, 49
Iowa...151
Irving, Washington...........................65, 66
Izard, Ralph.................................. 91
Jefferson, Joseph.............................. 94
Joinville, Prince de........................... 67
Joliet... 17
Jumonville.................................... 18
Jusserand..................................8, 196
Kaskaskia, 13, 17, 21–23, 25–27, 29, 39, 43, 97, 132, 138
Lacassagne....................................139
La Chaise...................................... 31
Lafayette, 65, 71, 75, 95, 104, 142, 187, 188, 190, 194
Lafitte, Jean.................................50, 51
Lafitte, Pierre 50, 162

INDEX

"Lafitte, Pierre and Jean, Historical Sketch of"
(Gayarré).................................50, 51
Lakanal.................44, 159, 161, 163, 166, 181
Lalande.. 45
Lallemand................161, 162, 167, 181, 183
La Roche.. 32
La Rochefoucauld, Duc de, 94, 140, 142, 143, 145
    189, 208
La Salle......................13, 17, 18, 22, 35
Lassus...119
Lassus, De...................................... 48
Latour.......................................44, 51
Laussat.......................................40-42
Lauzun.. 65
Law, John.....................................15, 37
Le Braz, Anatole................................ 7
Le Contes, the.................................. 53
Lefebvre Desnouettes...............159, 162, 167
L'Enfant.......................68, 69, 71, 73
Lesueur.. 36
Lesueur, Charles........................209, 210
Lewis and Clark................................ 45
Lefever, Isaac................................. 58
Lehigh, country................................ 60
Lezay Marnezia.................................119
Liancourt, Rochefoucauld................191, 205
Lodge.. 10
Louisiana....7, 10, 12, 15, 17, 30, 32, 33, 35-39, 41-43
——— Holy Inquisition in....................... 49
"Louisiana: A Record of Expansion" (A. Phelps). 46
"Louisiana Sugar Plantation of the Old Régime, A"
    (Gayarré)................................ 48
Louis XIV..................................33, 35
Louis Philippe, 11, 39, 143, 167, 168, 169, 174, 181
    182, 206, 208

230

INDEX

Louisville...........................29, 85, 89, 98, 139
Lucas...139
Luzerne............................72, 75, 187, 190
———— County.....................................145
Maison Rouge, Marquis de...................45, 48
Manakintown on the James......................14
Marengo, County, Alabama..................78, 161
Marie Antoinette.............................29, 64
Marietta.....................................29, 84
Marion, Francis.............................53, 93
Marquette.......................................17
Massac, Fort................................22, 25
Maurepas, Lake..................................36
Mazyck, Isaac...................................91
"Memorials of the Huguenots" (Stapleton) 57
Mexico.......................................32, 44
Michaux...31
Michigan..13
Mifflin, Fort...................................77
Milford, Pike County, Pennsylvania..............62
Miró, Governor 49
Mississippi Territory, the.....................171
Mobile....................................14, 26, 37
Monette, John W ....19 note
Monongahela, the..............................116
Monroe County, Pennsylvania....................62
Montgomery, E...................................88
Montpensier, Duc de...........................208
Moreau....................26, 44, 82, 178, 208
Morris, Gouverneur 106–108, 206
Morris, Mrs. Robert...........................206
Motte...93
"Mount Desert" (G. E. Street)..................32
Muskingum, the 18
Napoleon, 8, 12, 32, 40–42, 44, 166, 174, 178, 180,
    181, 203

INDEX

"New France and New England" (Fiske).......... 33

New Madrid....................................... 24

New Orleans, 16, 17, 22, 23, 27, 37, 39, 44, 47, 49, 82

New Rochelle...........................53, 55, 56

Noailles, Vicomte de, 40, 68, 71, 72, 82, 99, 129, 141,
    142, 143, 144, 146, 148, 202, 208

Ohio 18, 29

Ohio, the....18, 20, 22, 29, 30, 116, 125, 128, 129, 171

Ohio Company, the 20, 29, 133, 136, 137, 138

Old French Road, the 145

Old French War, the..................... 19, 133

Paine, "Tom"...................................... 65

Paris, Comte de................................... 67

Paris, Kentucky..............................78, 98

Parkman..7, 17

Parrish, Randall................................. 21

Patriotic Society, the French 77

Penn... 53

Penn's early settlers............................. 59

Pensacola... 39

Peoria.. 24

Peorias, the 22

Perin.. 46

Phelps, Albert................................... 46

Philadelphia, 20, 48, 59, 66, 68, 72–74, 77, 78, 81, 82,
    83, 86, 87, 89, 137

Philippe, St.............................23, 25, 27

Philosophical Society, the American, 8, 82, 139, 186,
    190, 193–196, 198, 203, 209

Pike's Expedition................................. 45

Pinchot, Constantine............................. 62

Polony, Dr....................................... 94

Pontalba.. 40

Pontchartrain, Lake.............................. 36

Pontgibaud, Chevalier de....................76, 196

Poydras... 39

INDEX

Prairie du Chien.............................152
Prairie du Pont.......................... 23
Pratz, Le Page du............................ 37
Prioleau, Rev. Elias.......................... 92
Puisaye......................................101
Quincy....................................... 24
Ravenel, Mrs. St. Julien.....................91 note
Raynal, Abbé................................. 79
Rayneval, Gerard de..........................187
"Relations et Memoires Inédits" (Margry)......... 33
"Reminiscences of Wilmington, Delaware" (E.
    Montgomery)............................... 88
Renault......................................23–25
Revere, Paul.................................53, 54
Robert....................................... 93
Roberval..................................... 32
Robin.......................................43, 45
Robin's "Travels,".....................45 note
Robin's voyage to Louisiana.................... 43
Rochambeau 10, 40, 64, 65, 72, 77, 81, 83, 208
Rocher, Prairie du..........22, 23, 25, 27, 43, 97, 132
Rock Island.................................. 24
Roosevelt...................................7, 26, 28
Roosevelt's "Winning of the West".....19, 26, 28 note
Scioto Company, the ..20, 21, 29, 46, 84, 134, 136, 137
Scioto County, Ohio........................... 31
Sedella, Antonio de..........................49, 50
Segur.. 64
Sigourneys, the 54
Stapleton.................................... 57
St. Castine, Baron de......................... 33
St. Domingo..................................86, 93
Ste. Genevieve............................... 97
St. Ildefonso, Treaty of...................... 40
St. Louis..............22, 38, 43, 85, 97, 132, 138, 158
St. Louis, Fort..........................22, 25, 35

INDEX

St. Vincent..138
Street, George E.................................. 32
Talleyrand,...........82, 198, 200, 201, 202, 204, 208
Talleyrand Perigord.........................190, 192
Talon, Omer......82, 99, 142, 144, 145, 146, 148, 150
Tardiveau.......................................28, 139
Texas..32, 35
Tombigbee Association, the 174
Tonti.. 13
Toussard.....................................73, 77
Trouillard, Rev. Florente Philippe................ 92
Ulloa.. 16
Uniontown, Pennsylvania......................... 18
University of Louisiana, the 166
Vergennes...............................121, 188, 190
Versailles, Kentucky.........................78, 98
Victor, General................................... 40
Vigo, Francis..................................... 29
Villiers, Jean Jules Le Moyne de................133
Vincennes........15, 17, 19, 21, 24, 26–28, 43, 97, 131
Virginia Company, the 18
Volney, 82, 129, 130, 132, 136, 137, 138, 190, 192, 198
    204, 208
Vrain, St....................................... 48
Wabash, the 21, 28, 131
Walbach, Gen. John de......................... 90
Walbach, Rev. Louis Barth de................... 89
Warren, Pennsylvania.......................... 18
Washington, George 18, 64, 70, 71, 80, 200, 208
Washita, the 45, 48
Western Pennsylvania.......................61, 63
West Virginia................................... 18
Wheeling Creek................................. 18
"Wilmington, Delaware, Reminiscences of" (E.
    Montgomery)................................ 88
"Winning of The West" (Roosevelt's)..19, 26, 28 note

French Colonists and Exiles
in the United States